# I call you

Master, where do you live?
Come and see.

## Gospel of Luke

### psalms, prayers

Publisher       Éditions Anne Sigier
1073, boul. René-Lévesque Ouest
Sillery (Québec) G1S 4R5
Canada

On the cover     *The Calling of the Apostles Peter and Andrew*,
by Duccio di Buoninsegna,
Samuel H. Kress Collection © 1997, Board of Trustees,
National Gallery of Art, Washington

ISBN       2-89129-292-8

Legal deposit    3rd quarter 1997
Bibliothèque nationale du Québec
National Library of Canada

*To Pope John Paul II*

This book as an answer to his call,

"May the Word of God become more familiar to you,
because it is the preferred way for the flowering of vocations."

*World Vocation Day*

| Publisher | Éditions Anne Sigier<br>1073, boul. René-Lévesque Ouest<br>Sillery (Québec) G1S 4R5<br>Canada |
|---|---|
| On the cover | *The Calling of the Apostles Peter and Andrew*,<br>by Duccio di Buoninsegna,<br>Samuel H. Kress Collection © 1997, Board of Trustees,<br>National Gallery of Art, Washington |
| ISBN | 2-89129-292-8 |
| Legal deposit | 3rd quarter 1997<br>Bibliothèque nationale du Québec<br>National Library of Canada |

You are searching for your way in life, you aspire for truth, you want to live. This book attempts to meet your expectations.

Listen to the Word, it will become the place where you will meet Jesus Christ. He is the Way, the Truth, and the Life, the one you are looking for.

In this Gospel, Jesus speaks about you when he says, "Happy are you who weep now... Love your enemies... Do not judge others... Yours sins are forgiven... This is my body, which is given for you... I am with you always until the end of time."

No part of your life is unknown to God: your joys, your sorrows. He carries with you what hurts you, he understands your doubts, he knows about your despair and your sin, he who is all mercy and forgiveness. "Get up and walk", says God, who calls you by your name.

To be able to offer you this book, we have had the support from the religious congregations, the pastors and the faithful. The Church, in Canada like everywhere else, is aware of the importance of evangelization. We believe that, beyond the restlessness in the world, beyond deceit and power, beyond war and money, there exists a safe reference: Jesus Christ in his Word and in the sacraments.

*I call you*: the title of the book is important. Indeed, we are convinced that, today as always, God calls, and that his voice will be heard in silence and in prayer, far from the noises and deceptions which make one wander away from God, losing all meaning in life.

This book will establish a communion between the youth of all countries, to whom the Pope, our beloved pastor, was saying, "The Church needs you to bring to the world the good news of the Gospel. She needs the witness of your hope and of your fervour to help her fulfill her mission. From Christ, who is the head of the Church, you receive his Word of truth, his own life, the breath of love which will allow you to love him faithfully and to have a successful life because you risk it by giving it joyfully for others."

Pray for us just as we pray for you, and may Jesus' prayer to his Father become reality: "... so that they may have life, and life everlasting."

*ANNE SIGIER*
*and the editorial team*

We would like to thank Mgr Renato Boccardo and Mgr Michel Dubost, who have looked favorably upon this project for evangelization and vocations.

# A LETTER TO YOU

I decided to begin this letter with a Hindu tale which has had a great influence over my own life. I hope that it will summarize all that I am trying to tell you in this letter. It goes like this:

*A fiancé returned after a long trip abroad. He arrived in his village just as nightfall was approaching. He proceeded directly to his fiancée's house and knocked at her door. His fiancée was just on her way to bed; troubled, she responded:*

*- Who is there?*

*Her fiancé cried out:*

*- It's me!*

*He rapped on the door a second time. But the door remained closed.*

*- It's me! repeated her fiancé. It's me!*

*Still the door did not open. In anger and tears, her fiancé, disappointed, became still. After having reflected a few moments, he softly knocked on the door for the third time.*

*- Who is there? asked his fiancée.*

*Then, respectfully, her fiancé murmured:*

*- It's you!*

*And the door opened.*

Where are you headed to? In which direction are you going?

You talk to me about your school studies, your work, even your worries and preoccupations. You tell me about your travels and outings. I am glad that you have confided in me. However, please excuse me if I say that you are not going to the heart of things.

Listen: school, work – these are but means to an end. Evidently, you must earn a living, you must be successful in your studies.

But in order to do what? What is the real goal? Do you want to make money? Rise above others so that you can exercise your power over them?

At the heart of all of this, it is really yourself that you are looking for.

I know that you must have a career, that leaders are necessary, and, even, that having money is indispensable. But let's talk seriously: these are realities that don't run very deep; we are still talking about means to an end. In carrying out responsibilities, it is very tempting to get ahead by taking advantage of others. There is terrible ambiguity in this reasoning – everyone's reasoning – and therefore the anonymous reasoning of no one. Do you wish to live your life in an anonymous society with limited responsibility? I repeat my question: what is at the heart of all this? the essential truth?

For a time, I was involved in looking after wills. I was stupefied to discover the amount of money left behind by ordinary people upon their death. They hadn't even benefited from their riches. Why all this money? Why hold on to it? Out of fear of not having enough. And so many others who hold power over those around them, arbitrary power. What motivates them? What force incites them to carry on like household tyrants, like despots in the classroom or at the workplace? The desire to assert themselves out of fear of not being important enough.

These lives are driven by fear: fear of not having enough, fear of precariousness. Therefore, they keep and protect, accumulate and hold back. They imprison themselves in fortresses, like the Tower of Babel. Against what enemy? Against death. It is, in reality, death that rules this game and everything one does is done to protect oneself from death. A fearsome game that imprisons so many men.

If you allow your life to be influenced by this disaster, then you have no need for Jesus Christ. If you use your freedom only for superficial means, even for a religious cause, you harbour an empty, meaningless life. You remain centered on yourself.

However, if you want your life to become a source of life, then let Christ become the center of your life. If you are seeking a breath of fresh air full of generosity, open your door to Christ. Entrust your life into his hands. He will bring new meaning to your life. Death will no longer rule your life. Life will flow out of you. You will live in Christ today. This is the hope that he is offering you.

"If you want to save your own life, you will lose it, but if you lose your life for my sake, you will save it." (Matt. 10: 39)

"Yet it is no longer I, but Christ living in me." (Gal. 2: 20)

They say that people today don't seem to need Christ. This is not surprising. What are the needs which are valued in today's society? What is man seeking?

As long as the rich desire to become richer, leaving the poor to become poorer, they have no need for Christ. As long as businessmen play the deadly competitive game of hoping to obtain, if possible, the entire market for themselves, dreaming of being alone – like Adam before the coming of Eve – they have no need for Christ. As long as love means taking advantage of the other, there is no need for Christ. Or rather, Christ is present, crucified.

Silent and exposed, he shows the world what men are capable of doing to the Son of Man.

Living is more than just this!

Men have become imprisoned by the very economic laws they have invented. And they are then surprised by the consequences of their actions, and try to correct their errors. And, silent, on the cross, Christ reflects the faces of malnourished children, of broken men. He represents all those who are silent. The world is groaning under the heavy weight of a system which places more value on things, mere objects, than on mankind.

And you would like Christ to come and approve of such a situation? That he approve of so much inhumanity?

The rich young man was suffocating from having obeyed all of God's commandments (cf. Luke 18: 18-23). He was moralistic and even virtuous. However, all of this did not guarantee him a worthy life. Christ answered him, "You want to live a truly rich life? Give." Because your life is not measured by how much you have , but by how much you give.

If you want to truly live, be generous. You will be "a child of the resurrection" (Luke 20: 36).

❇

Can you see that in order to become less preoccupied with yourself and to live, the path to Christ is essential. He is the Living. He offers you life.

You say that this program interests you, but that the Church interests you less so. Note that this reflection stills leaves you in a good position! Because "being interested in Christ," as you say, can become just another egotistical but religious way of putting oneself first! All right then, let's talk about the Church.

It is very surprising to realize how much we talk more about the images of the Church than of its reality. These images are not always flattering. They allow us to see only the surface, just as our skin does. Therefore, we are given the impression that the Church is an association, a kind of club that anyone who wants to can enter, and by whichever door he chooses.

In other words, each individual sees the Church from his own point of view. And, as the fiancé in the Hindu tale, repeats, "It's me! It's me!"

The Church is the body where Christ brings us all together. People who don't normally talk to each other hear the same Word. People who wouldn't normally invite each other for lunch share the same Bread. It is not us who make the Church, it is Christ who brings us together, reunites us. "He sanctifies and cleanses it," said Saint Paul. (Eph. 5: 26-29)

Christ takes us into him and makes us "all members one of another" (Eph. 4: 25). We are all related to one another by the most intimate link of all: faith and confidence in Christ.

When you celebrate mass, you begin by saying, "Lord, have mercy." We know that we are, each one of us in our own way, unworthy members of the Church. Peter himself betrayed, Judas betrayed his master, and the other ten ran away. That is our point of departure, with all its concrete humanity, yours, mine. Or rather, no! the true starting point is the forgiveness of Christ: forgiveness to Peter by entrusting him with the charge of the sheep, forgiveness accorded to the apostles. We are the Church of the son lost, the son found. Never-ending.

If God was waiting until we were perfect to work with us, he would be waiting a long time! However, the wonderful thing is that he is willing to work with us and calls us to him as we are. His calling attracts us and pushes us forward. The Church is called by this voice that has confidence in man: the never-ending hope of God.

At this point, I am brought to think of all the many young people for whom life has no meaning. In a world of objects and money, they cannot find anyone to talk to. Their isolation weighs so heavily on them – I mean their isolation from the essential things – that their existence falls into emptiness. "I no longer have a taste for life," wrote a young girl before she ended it all. I know a little of the mystery that lives inside the freewill of each one of us. But, getting back to "taste," you will remember that the word "Gospel" means "Good News": a matter of taste. In this way, Christ asks us, of you and of I, to be the salt of the Earth, to give taste to it by becoming closer to others.

The Church is a place of hope. Yes, our weak and heavy humanity is transfixed with the Spirit of Christ. He calls upon us to love. He trusts us. He has given us a planet to humanize, a Gospel to spread, a life to multiply. Together, as brothers, invited to accept one another, called upon to love one another. The Church provides a sign of the hope of God for humanity. That is essentially the heart of it.

"And a hope which will not let us down, because the love of God has been poured into our hearts by the Holy Spirit which has been given to us" (Rom. 5: 5).

❉

A word comes to mind: "leniency." It is a word we seldom hear, and that is unfortunate. For it describes an attitude of confidence which forgives, openness of mind that hopes, and tender generosity that accompanies us. For me, it is a word that defines the Church, a Church that Christ gives us and a Church that each of us must serve in his own way from our own place in life.

Essentially, everything that I am writing to you can be summed up in terms of a turnaround, a "conversion." Please forgive me if, in this letter, I introduce a somewhat technical distinction, but I don't know how I can explain this otherwise. The New Testament differentiates between two types of conversions.

The first type of conversion involves turning one's back on a fixed goal, going backwards, because you recognize that you have made a mistake somewhere along the way. "Burn what you have worshipped, worship what you have burned," proclaimed Saint Rémi, Bishop of Reims, while baptizing King Clovis.

We can clearly see what this type of conversion means: turning yourself away from evil and embracing good. This in itself is a lot, but it is not enough.

I know people who have held onto their notion of what is good. They have made a conversion while keeping their own compass bearings intact. In general, their personal world changes little. This process sometimes renders them very uncompromising.

The other type of conversion is at a level so profound that one's mentality changes, one's way of thinking evolves. It is like taking a new compass, with a different bearing. In this case, Christ sets the direction we want to move in. The Spirit is the light guiding our thoughts and the Father becomes the center of our lives. It is another world, real life. One lives as though outside of oneself in Christ resurrected. Therefore, we are really "a new creation: the old order in gone and a new being is there to see" (2 Cor. 5:17).

It is no longer I that comes first, but "You," Christ. It is no longer death and its ambiguity that leads my life, but rather resurrection through sharing. In my body, mind and soul, a new being is about to be born. In order to allow this new being to emerge, I was created and put into the world free of will, because God wants me to participate in this springing up.

I then discover that the history of the world is not an absurd, empty shell, full of misery, injustice, anger and cries, but that it does have real meaning. Christ lifted up from the earth draws all people to him. As I said, he draws them, he does not control them. Such is the boundless hope that God places is us: to participate in his work so that the creation can be reborn again in Christ.

❄

Yes we are weak and small, but God is greater than our spirit. His hope will carry us. For it brings us to the logic of God, a generosity never-ending.

I wanted to tell you all of these things, for God calls on you to enter into this beauty. This is your calling. Redirecting your life in this way will bring you an inner peace and joy that, as Jesus said, "no man can take from you" (John 16: 22). This is the life I wish for you, in a spirit of true brotherly love.

Very best wishes!

☩ *Albert Rouet*
*Bishop of Poitiers*

# THE GOSPEL
# ACCORDING
# TO LUKE

"My Lord and my God."
Painting by Kiko Arguëllo

## INTRODUCTION

1 Dear Theophilus:
 Many people have done their best to write a report of the things that have taken place among us. [2]They wrote what we have been told by those who saw these things from the beginning and who proclaimed the message. [3]And so, Your Excellency, because I have carefully studied all these matters from their beginning, I thought it would be good to write an orderly account for you. [4]I do this so that you will know the full truth about everything which you have been taught.

## THE BIRTH OF JOHN THE BAPTIST IS ANNOUNCED

[5]During the time when Herod was king of Judea, there was a priest named Zechariah, who belonged to the priestly order of Abijah. His wife's name was Elizabeth; she also belonged to a priestly family. [6]They both lived good lives in God's sight and obeyed fully all the Lord's laws and commands. [7]They had no children because Elizabeth could not have any, and she and Zechariah were both very old.

[8]One day Zechariah was doing his work as a priest in the Temple, taking his turn in the daily service. [9]According to the custom followed by the priests, he was chosen by lot to burn incense on the altar. So he went into the Temple of the Lord, [10]while the crowd of people outside prayed during the hour when the incense was burned. [11]An angel of the Lord appeared to him, standing at the right side of the altar where the incense was burned. [12]When Zechariah saw him, he was alarmed and felt afraid. [13]But the angel said to him, "Don't be afraid, Zechariah! God has heard your prayer, and your wife Elizabeth will bear you a son. You are to name him John. [14]How glad and happy you will be, and how happy many others will be when he is born! [15]John will be great in the Lord's sight. He must not drink any wine or strong drink. From his very birth he will be filled with the Holy Spirit, [16]and he will bring back many of the people of Israel to the Lord their God. [17]He will go ahead of the Lord, strong and mighty like the prophet Elijah. He will bring fathers and children together again; he will turn disobedient people back to the way of thinking of the righteous; he will get the Lord's people ready for him."

[18]Zechariah said to the angel, "How shall I know if this is so? I am an old man, and my wife is old also."

[19]"I am Gabriel," the angel answered. "I stand in the presence of God, who sent me to speak to you and tell you this good news. [20]But you have not believed my message, which will come true at the right time. Because you have not believed, you will be unable to speak; you will remain silent until the day my promise to you comes true."

[21]In the meantime the people were waiting for Zechariah and wondering why he was spending such a long time in the Temple. [22]When he came out, he could not speak to them, and so they knew that he had seen a vision in the Temple. Unable to say a word, he made signs to them with his hands.

[23]When his period of service in the Temple was over, Zechariah went back home. [24]Some time later his wife Elizabeth became pregnant and did not leave the house for five months. [25]"Now at last the Lord has helped me," she said. "He has taken away my public disgrace!"

## THE BIRTH OF JESUS IS ANNOUNCED

[26]In the sixth month of Elizabeth's pregnancy God sent the angel Gabriel to a town in Galilee named Nazareth. [27]He had a message for a young woman promised in marriage to a man named Joseph, who was a descendant of King David. Her name was Mary.

²⁸The angel came to her and said, "Peace be with you! The Lord is with you and has greatly blessed you!"

²⁹Mary was deeply troubled by the angel's message, and she wondered what his words meant. ³⁰The angel said to her, "Don't be afraid, Mary; God has been gracious to you. ³¹You will become pregnant and give birth to a son, and you will name him Jesus. ³²He will be great and will be called the Son of the Most High God. The Lord God will make him a king, as his ancestor David was, ³³and he will be the king of the descendants of Jacob forever; his kingdom will never end!"

³⁴Mary said to the angel, "I am a virgin. How, then, can this be?"

³⁵The angel answered, "The Holy Spirit will come on you, and God's power will rest upon you. For this reason the holy child will be called the Son of God. ³⁶Remember your relative Elizabeth. It is said that she cannot have children, but she herself is now six months pregnant, even though she is very old. ³⁷For there is nothing that God cannot do."

³⁸"I am the Lord's servant," said Mary; "may it happen to me as you have said." And the angel left her.

## MARY VISITS ELIZABETH

³⁹Soon afterward Mary got ready and hurried off to a town in the hill country of Judea. ⁴⁰She went into Zechariah's house and greeted Elizabeth. ⁴¹When Elizabeth heard Mary's greeting, the baby moved within her. Elizabeth was filled with the Holy Spirit ⁴²and said in a loud voice, "You are the most blessed of all women, and blessed is the child you will bear! ⁴³Why should this great thing happen to me, that my Lord's mother comes to visit me? ⁴⁴For as soon as I heard your greeting, the baby within me jumped with gladness. ⁴⁵How happy you are to believe that the Lord's message to you will come true!"

## MARY'S SONG OF PRAISE

⁴⁶Mary said,

"My heart praises the Lord;
⁴⁷my soul is glad because of God
my Savior,
⁴⁸for he has remembered me,
his lowly servant!
From now on all people
will call me happy,
⁴⁹because of the great things
the Mighty God has done for me.
His name is holy;
⁵⁰from one generation to another
he shows mercy to those
who honor him.
⁵¹He has stretched out
his mighty arm
and scattered the proud
with all their plans.
⁵²He has brought down mighty kings
from their thrones,
and lifted up the lowly.
⁵³He has filled the hungry
with good things,
and sent the rich away
with empty hands.
⁵⁴He has kept the promise
he made to our ancestors,
and has come to the help
of his servant Israel.
⁵⁵He has remembered to show mercy
to Abraham
and to all his descendants forever!"

⁵⁶Mary stayed about three months with Elizabeth and then went back home.

## THE BIRTH OF JOHN THE BAPTIST

⁵⁷The time came for Elizabeth to have her baby, and she gave birth to a son. ⁵⁸Her neighbors and relatives heard how wonderfully good the Lord had been to her, and they all rejoiced with her.

⁵⁹When the baby was a week old, they came to circumcise him, and they were going to name him Zechariah,

after his father. 60But his mother said, "No! His name is to be John."

61They said to her, "But you don't have any relative with that name!" 62Then they made signs to his father, asking him what name he would like the boy to have.

63Zechariah asked for a writing pad and wrote, "His name is John." How surprised they all were! 64At that moment Zechariah was able to speak again, and he started praising God. 65The neighbors were all filled with fear, and the news about these things spread through all the hill country of Judea. 66Everyone who heard of it thought about it and asked, "What is this child going to be?" For it was plain that the Lord's power was upon him.

## ZECHARIAH'S PROPHECY

67John's father Zechariah was filled with the Holy Spirit, and he spoke God's message:

68"Let us praise the Lord,
the God of Israel!
He has come to the help
of his people and has set them free.
69He has provided for us
a mighty Savior,
a descendant of his servant David.
70He promised through his holy
prophets long ago
71that he would save us
from our enemies,
from the power of all those
who hate us.
72He said he would show mercy
to our ancestors
and remember his sacred covenant.
73-74With a solemn oath
to our ancestor Abraham
he promised to rescue us
from our enemies
and allow us to serve him
without fear,
75so that we might be holy
and righteous before him
all the days of our life.

76"You, my child, will be called
a prophet of the Most High God.
You will go ahead of the Lord
to prepare his road for him,
77to tell his people
that they will be saved
by having their sins forgiven.
78Our God is merciful and tender.
He will cause the bright dawn
of salvation to rise on us
79and to shine from heaven
on all those who live
in the dark shadow of death,
to guide our steps
into the path of peace."

80The child grew and developed in body and spirit. He lived in the desert until the day when he appeared publicly to the people of Israel.

## THE BIRTH OF JESUS

2 At that time Emperor Augustus ordered a census to be taken throughout the Roman Empire. 2When this first census took place, Quirinius was the governor of Syria. 3Everyone, then, went to register himself, each to his own hometown.

4Joseph went from the town of Nazareth in Galilee to the town of Bethlehem in Judea, the birthplace of King David. Joseph went there because he was a descendant of David. 5He went to register with Mary, who was promised in marriage to him. She was pregnant, 6and while they were in Bethlehem, the time came for her to have her baby. 7She gave birth to her first son, wrapped him in cloths and laid him in a manger–there was no room for them to stay in the inn.

## THE SHEPHERDS AND THE ANGELS

8There were some shepherds in that part of the country who were spending the night in the fields, taking care of their flocks. 9An angel of the Lord appeared to them, and the glory of the Lord shone over them. They were terribly afraid, [10]but the angel said to them, "Don't be afraid! I am here with good news for you, which will bring great joy to all the people. [11]This very day in David's town your Savior was born–Christ the Lord! [12]And this is what will prove it to you: you will find a baby wrapped in cloths and lying in a manger."

[13]Suddenly a great army of heaven's angels appeared with the angel, singing praises to God:

[14]"Glory to God
in the highest heaven,
and peace on earth to those
with whom he is pleased!"

[15]When the angels went away from them back into heaven, the shepherds said to one another, "Let's go to Bethlehem and see this thing that has happened, which the Lord has told us."

[16]So they hurried off and found Mary and Joseph and saw the baby lying in the manger. [17]When the shepherds saw him, they told them what the angel had said about the child. [18]All who heard it were amazed at what the shepherds said. [19]Mary remembered all these things and thought deeply about them. [20]The shepherds went back, singing praises to God for all they had heard and seen; it had been just as the angel had told them.

### JESUS IS NAMED

[21]A week later, when the time came for the baby to be circumcised, he was named Jesus, the name which the angel had given him before he had been conceived.

### JESUS IS PRESENTED IN THE TEMPLE

[22]The time came for Joseph and Mary to perform the ceremony of purification, as the Law of Moses commanded. So they took the child to Jerusalem to present him to the Lord, [23]as it is written in the law of the Lord: "Every first-born male is to be dedicated to the Lord." [24]They also went to offer a sacrifice of a pair of doves or two young pigeons, as required by the law of the Lord.

[25]At that time there was a man named Simeon living in Jerusalem. He was a good, God-fearing man and was waiting for Israel to be saved. The Holy Spirit was with him [26]and had assured him that he would not die before he had seen the Lord's promised Messiah. [27]Led by the Spirit, Simeon went into the Temple. When the parents brought the child Jesus into the Temple to do for him what the Law required, [28]Simeon took the child in his arms and gave thanks to God:

[29]"Now, Lord, you have kept
your promise,
and you may let your servant
go in peace.
[30]With my own eyes
I have seen your salvation,
[31]which you have prepared
in the presence of all peoples:
[32]A light to reveal your will
to the Gentiles
and bring glory
to your people Israel."

[33]The child's father and mother were amazed at the things Simeon said about him. [34]Simeon blessed them and said to Mary, his mother, "This child is chosen by God for the destruction and the salvation of many in Israel. He will be a sign from God which many people will speak against [35]and so reveal their secret thoughts. And sorrow, like a sharp sword, will break your own heart."

[36-37]There was a very old prophet, a widow named Anna, daughter of Phanuel of the tribe of Asher. She had been married for only seven years and was now eighty-four years old. She never left the Temple; day and night she worshiped God, fasting and praying. [38]That very same hour she arrived

and gave thanks to God and spoke about the child to all who were waiting for God to set Jerusalem free.

## The Return to Nazareth

³⁹When Joseph and Mary had finished doing all that was required by the Law of the Lord, they returned to their hometown of Nazareth in Galilee. ⁴⁰The child grew and became strong; he was full of wisdom, and God's blessings were upon him.

## The Boy Jesus in the Temple

⁴¹Every year the parents of Jesus went to Jerusalem for the Passover Festival. ⁴²When Jesus was twelve years old, they went to the festival as usual. ⁴³When the festival was over, they started back home, but the boy Jesus stayed in Jerusalem. His parents did not know this; ⁴⁴they thought that he was with the group, so they traveled a whole day and then started looking for him among their relatives and friends. ⁴⁵They did not find him, so they went back to Jerusalem looking for him. ⁴⁶On the third day they found him in the Temple, sitting with the Jewish teachers, listening to them and asking questions. ⁴⁷All who heard him were amazed at his intelligent answers. ⁴⁸His parents were astonished when they saw him, and his mother said to him, "Son, why have you done this to us? Your father and I have been terribly worried trying to find you."

⁴⁹He answered them, "Why did you have to look for me? Didn't you know that I had to be in my Father's house?" ⁵⁰But they did not understand his answer.

⁵¹So Jesus went back with them to Nazareth, where he was obedient to them. His mother treasured all these things in her heart. ⁵²Jesus grew both in body and in wisdom, gaining favor with God and people.

## The Preaching of John the Baptist

3 It was the fifteenth year of the rule of Emperor Tiberius; Pontius Pilate was governor of Judea, Herod was ruler of Galilee, and his brother Philip was ruler of the territory of Iturea and Trachonitis; Lysanias was ruler of Abilene, ²and Annas and Caiaphas were High Priests. At that time the word of God came to John son of Zechariah in the desert. ³So John went throughout the whole territory of the Jordan River, preaching, "Turn away from your sins and be baptized, and God will forgive your sins." ⁴As it is written in the book of the prophet Isaiah:

"Someone is shouting
   in the desert:
'Get the road ready for the Lord;
  make a straight path
    for him to travel!
⁵Every valley must be filled up,
every hill and mountain leveled off.
The winding roads
  must be made straight,
and the rough paths made smooth.
⁶The whole human race
  will see God's salvation!' "

⁷Crowds of people came out to John to be baptized by him. "You snakes!" he said to them. "Who told you that you could escape from the punishment God is about to send? ⁸Do those things that will show that you have turned from your sins. And don't start saying among yourselves that Abraham is your ancestor. I tell you that God can take these rocks and make descendants for Abraham! ⁹The ax is ready to cut down the trees at the roots; every tree that does not bear good fruit will be cut down and thrown in the fire."

¹⁰The people asked him, "What are we to do, then?"

¹¹He answered, "Whoever has two shirts must give one to the man who

has none, and whoever has food must share it."

[12]Some tax collectors came to be baptized, and they asked him, "Teacher, what are we to do?"

[13]"Don't collect more than is legal," he told them.

[14]Some soldiers also asked him, "What about us? What are we to do?"

He said to them, "Don't take money from anyone by force or accuse anyone falsely. Be content with your pay."

[15]People's hopes began to rise, and they began to wonder whether John perhaps might be the Messiah. [16]So John said to all of them, "I baptize you with water, but someone is coming who is much greater than I am. I am not good enough even to untie his sandals. He will baptize you with the Holy Spirit and fire. [17]He has his winnowing shovel with him, to thresh out all the grain and gather the wheat into his barn; but he will burn the chaff in a fire that never goes out."

[18]In many different ways John preached the Good News to the people and urged them to change their ways. [19]But John reprimanded Governor Herod, because he had married Herodias, his brother's wife, and had done many other evil things. [20]Then Herod did an even worse thing by putting John in prison.

### THE BAPTISM OF JESUS

[21]After all the people had been baptized, Jesus also was baptized. While he was praying, heaven was opened, [22]and the Holy Spirit came down upon him in bodily form like a dove. And a voice came from heaven, "You are my own dear Son. I am pleased with you."

### THE ANCESTORS OF JESUS

[23]When Jesus began his work, he was about thirty years old. He was the son, so people thought, of Joseph, who was the son of Heli, [24]the son of Matthat, the son of Levi, the son of Melchi, the son of Jannai, the son of Joseph, [25]the son of Mattathias, the son of Amos, the son of Nahum, the son of Esli, the son of Naggai, [26]the son of Maath, the son of Mattathias, the son of Semein, the son of Josech, the son of Joda, [27]the son of Joanan, the son of Rhesa, the son of Zerubbabel, the son of Shealtiel, the son of Neri, [28]the son of Melchi, the son of Addi, the son of Cosam, the son of Elmadam, the son of Er, [29]the son of Joshua, the son of Eliezer, the son of Jorim, the son of Matthat, the son of Levi, [30]the son of Simeon, the son of Judah, the son of Joseph, the son of Jonam, the son of Eliakim, [31]the son of Melea, the son of Menna, the son of Mattatha, the son of Nathan, the son of David, [32]the son of Jesse, the son of Obed, the son of Boaz, the son of Salmon, the son of Nahshon, [33]the son of Amminadab, the son of Admin, the son of Arni, the son of Hezron, the son of Perez, the son of Judah, [34]the son of Jacob, the son of Isaac, the son of Abraham, the son of Terah, the son of Nahor, [35]the son of Serug, the son of Reu, the son of Peleg, the son of Eber, the son of Shelah, [36]the son of Cainan, the son of Arphaxad, the son of Shem, the son of Noah, the son of Lamech, [37]the son of Methuselah, the son of Enoch, the son of Jared, the son of Mahalaleel, the son of Kenan, [38]the son of Enosh, the son of Seth, the son of Adam, the son of God.

### THE TEMPTATION OF JESUS

4 Jesus returned from the Jordan full of the Holy Spirit and was led by the Spirit into the desert, [2]where he was tempted by the Devil for forty days. In all that time he ate nothing, so that he was hungry when it was over.

³The Devil said to him, "If you are God's Son, order this stone to turn into bread."

⁴But Jesus answered, "The scripture says, 'Human beings cannot live on bread alone.'"

⁵Then the Devil took him up and showed him in a second all the kingdoms of the world. ⁶"I will give you all this power and all this wealth," the Devil told him. "It has all been handed over to me, and I can give it to anyone I choose. ⁷All this will be yours, then, if you worship me."

⁸Jesus answered, "The scripture says, 'Worship the Lord your God and serve only him!'"

⁹Then the Devil took him to Jerusalem and set him on the highest point of the Temple, and said to him, "If you are God's Son, throw yourself down from here. ¹⁰For the scripture says, 'God will order his angels to take good care of you.' ¹¹It also says, 'They will hold you up with their hands so that not even your feet will be hurt on the stones.'"

¹²But Jesus answered, "The scripture says, 'Do not put the Lord your God to the test.'"

¹³When the Devil finished tempting Jesus in every way, he left him for a while.

### JESUS BEGINS HIS WORK IN GALILEE

¹⁴Then Jesus returned to Galilee, and the power of the Holy Spirit was with him. The news about him spread throughout all that territory. ¹⁵He taught in the synagogues and was praised by everyone.

### JESUS IS REJECTED AT NAZARETH

¹⁶Then Jesus went to Nazareth, where he had been brought up, and on the Sabbath he went as usual to the synagogue. He stood up to read the Scriptures ¹⁷and was handed the book of the prophet Isaiah. He unrolled the scroll and found the place where it is written,

¹⁸"The Spirit of the Lord
    is upon me,
because he has chosen me
to bring good news to the poor.
He has sent me to proclaim
    liberty to the captives
and recovery of sight to the blind,
    to set free the oppressed
¹⁹and announce
    that the time has come
when the Lord will save his people."

²⁰Jesus rolled up the scroll, gave it back to the attendant, and sat down. All the people in the synagogue had their eyes fixed on him, ²¹as he said to them, "This passage of scripture has come true today, as you heard it being read."

²²They were all well impressed with him and marveled at the eloquent words that he spoke. They said, "Isn't he the son of Joseph?"

²³He said to them, "I am sure that you will quote this proverb to me, 'Doctor, heal yourself.' You will also tell me to do here in my hometown the same things you heard were done in Capernaum. ²⁴I tell you this," Jesus added, "prophets are never welcomed in their hometown. ²⁵Listen to me: it is true that there were many widows in Israel during the time of Elijah, when there was no rain for three and a half years and a severe famine spread throughout the whole land. ²⁶Yet Elijah was not sent to anyone in Israel, but only to a widow living in Zarephath in the territory of Sidon. ²⁷And there were many people suffering from a dreaded skin disease who lived in Israel during the time of the prophet Elisha; yet not one of them was healed, but only Naaman the Syrian."

²⁸When the people in the synagogue heard this, they were filled with anger. ²⁹They rose up, dragged Jesus out of town, and took him to the top of the

hill on which their town was built. They meant to throw him over the cliff, [30]but he walked through the middle of the crowd and went his way.

### A MAN WITH AN EVIL SPIRIT

[31]Then Jesus went to Capernaum, a town in Galilee, where he taught the people on the Sabbath. [32]They were all amazed at the way he taught, because he spoke with authority. [33]In the synagogue was a man who had the spirit of an evil demon in him; he screamed out in a loud voice, [34]"Ah! What do you want with us, Jesus of Nazareth? Are you here to destroy us? I know who you are: you are God's holy messenger!"

[35]Jesus ordered the spirit, "Be quiet and come out of the man!" The demon threw the man down in front of them and went out of him without doing him any harm.

[36]The people were all amazed and said to one another, "What kind of words are these? With authority and power this man gives orders to the evil spirits, and they come out!" [37]And the report about Jesus spread everywhere in that region.

### JESUS HEALS MANY PEOPLE

[38]Jesus left the synagogue and went to Simon's home. Simon's mother-in-law was sick with a high fever, and they spoke to Jesus about her. [39]He went and stood at her bedside and ordered the fever to leave her. The fever left her, and she got up at once and began to wait on them.

[40]After sunset all who had friends who were sick with various diseases brought them to Jesus; he placed his hands on every one of them and healed them all. [41]Demons also went out from many people, screaming, "You are the Son of God!"

Jesus gave the demons an order and would not let them speak, because they knew he was the Messiah.

### JESUS PREACHES IN THE SYNAGOGUES

[42]At daybreak Jesus left the town and went off to a lonely place. The people started looking for him, and when they found him, they tried to keep him from leaving. [43]But he said to them, "I must preach the Good News about the Kingdom of God in other towns also, because that is what God sent me to do."

[44]So he preached in the synagogues throughout the country.

### JESUS CALLS THE FIRST DISCIPLES

5 One day Jesus was standing on the shore of Lake Gennesaret while the people pushed their way up to him to listen to the word of God. [2]He saw two boats pulled up on the beach; the fishermen had left them and were washing the nets. [3]Jesus got into one of the boats–it belonged to Simon–and asked him to push off a little from the shore. Jesus sat in the boat and taught the crowd.

[4]When he finished speaking, he said to Simon, "Push the boat out further to the deep water, and you and your partners let down your nets for a catch."

[5]"Master," Simon answered, "we worked hard all night long and caught nothing. But if you say so, I will let down the nets." [6]They let them down and caught such a large number of fish that the nets were about to break. [7]So they motioned to their partners in the other boat to come and help them. They came and filled both boats so full of fish that the boats were about to sink. [8]When Simon Peter saw what had happened, he fell on his knees before Jesus and said, "Go away from me, Lord! I am a sinful man!"

[9]He and the others with him were all amazed at the large number of fish

they had caught. [10]The same was true of Simon's partners, James and John, the sons of Zebedee. Jesus said to Simon, "Don't be afraid; from now on you will be catching people."

[11]They pulled the boats up on the beach, left everything, and followed Jesus.

### JESUS HEALS A MAN

[12]Once Jesus was in a town where there was a man who was suffering from a dreaded skin disease. When he saw Jesus, he threw himself down and begged him, "Sir, if you want to, you can make me clean!"

[13]Jesus reached out and touched him. "I do want to," he answered. "Be clean!" At once the disease left the man. [14]Jesus ordered him, "Don't tell anyone, but go straight to the priest and let him examine you; then to prove to everyone that you are cured, offer the sacrifice as Moses ordered."

[15]But the news about Jesus spread all the more widely, and crowds of people came to hear him and be healed from their diseases. [16]But he would go away to lonely places, where he prayed.

### JESUS HEALS A PARALYZED MAN

[17]One day when Jesus was teaching, some Pharisees and teachers of the Law were sitting there who had come from every town in Galilee and Judea and from Jerusalem. The power of the Lord was present for Jesus to heal the sick. [18]Some men came carrying a paralyzed man on a bed, and they tried to carry him into the house and put him in front of Jesus. [19]Because of the crowd, however, they could find no way to take him in. So they carried him up on the roof, made an opening in the tiles, and let him down on his bed into the middle of the group in front of Jesus. [20]When Jesus saw how much faith they had, he said to the man, "Your sins are forgiven, my friend."

[21]The teachers of the Law and the Pharisees began to say to themselves, "Who is this man who speaks such blasphemy! God is the only one who can forgive sins!"

[22]Jesus knew their thoughts and said to them, "Why do you think such things? [23]Is it easier to say, 'Your sins are forgiven you,' or to say, 'Get up and walk'? [24]I will prove to you, then, that the Son of Man has authority on earth to forgive sins." So he said to the paralyzed man, "I tell you, get up, pick up your bed, and go home!"

[25]At once the man got up in front of them all, took the bed he had been lying on, and went home, praising God. [26]They were all completely amazed! Full of fear, they praised God, saying, "What marvelous things we have seen today!"

### JESUS CALLS LEVI

[27]After this, Jesus went out and saw a tax collector named Levi, sitting in his office. Jesus said to him, "Follow me." [28]Levi got up, left everything, and followed him.

[29]Then Levi had a big feast in his house for Jesus, and among the guests was a large number of tax collectors and other people. [30]Some Pharisees and some teachers of the Law who belonged to their group complained to Jesus' disciples. "Why do you eat and drink with tax collectors and other outcasts?" they asked.

[31]Jesus answered them, "People who are well do not need a doctor, but only those who are sick. [32]I have not come to call respectable people to repent, but outcasts."

### THE QUESTION ABOUT FASTING

[33]Some people said to Jesus, "The disciples of John fast frequently and offer prayers, and the disciples of the

Pharisees do the same; but your disciples eat and drink."

<sup>34</sup>Jesus answered, "Do you think you can make the guests at a wedding party go without food as long as the bridegroom is with them? Of course not! <sup>35</sup>But the day will come when the bridegroom will be taken away from them, and then they will fast."

<sup>36</sup>Jesus also told them this parable: "You don't tear a piece off a new coat to patch up an old coat. If you do, you will have torn the new coat, and the piece of new cloth will not match the old. <sup>37</sup>Nor do you pour new wine into used wineskins, because the new wine will burst the skins, the wine will pour out, and the skins will be ruined. <sup>38</sup>Instead, new wine must be poured into fresh wineskins! <sup>39</sup>And you don't want new wine after drinking old wine. 'The old is better,' you say."

### THE QUESTION ABOUT THE SABBATH

**6** Jesus was walking through some wheat fields on a Sabbath. His disciples began to pick the heads of wheat, rub them in their hands, and eat the grain. <sup>2</sup>Some Pharisees asked, "Why are you doing what our Law says you cannot do on the Sabbath?"

<sup>3</sup>Jesus answered them, "Haven't you read what David did when he and his men were hungry? <sup>4</sup>He went into the house of God, took the bread offered to God, ate it, and gave it also to his men. Yet it is against our Law for anyone except the priests to eat that bread."

<sup>5</sup>And Jesus concluded, "The Son of Man is Lord of the Sabbath."

### THE MAN WITH A PARALYZED HAND

<sup>6</sup>On another Sabbath Jesus went into a synagogue and taught. A man was there whose right hand was paralyzed. <sup>7</sup>Some teachers of the Law and some Pharisees wanted a reason to accuse Jesus of doing wrong, so they watched him closely to see if he would heal on the Sabbath. <sup>8</sup>But Jesus knew their thoughts and said to the man, "Stand up and come here to the front." The man got up and stood there. <sup>9</sup>Then Jesus said to them, "I ask you: What does our Law allow us to do on the Sabbath? To help or to harm? To save someone's life or destroy it?" <sup>10</sup>He looked around at them all; then he said to the man, "Stretch out your hand." He did so, and his hand became well again.

<sup>11</sup>They were filled with rage and began to discuss among themselves what they could do to Jesus.

### JESUS CHOOSES THE TWELVE APOSTLES

<sup>12</sup>At that time Jesus went up a hill to pray and spent the whole night there praying to God. <sup>13</sup>When day came, he called his disciples to him and chose twelve of them, whom he named apostles: <sup>14</sup>Simon (whom he named Peter) and his brother Andrew; James and John, Philip and Bartholomew, <sup>15</sup>Matthew and Thomas, James son of Alphaeus, and Simon (who was called the Patriot), <sup>16</sup>Judas son of James, and Judas Iscariot, who became the traitor.

### JESUS TEACHES AND HEALS

<sup>17</sup>When Jesus had come down from the hill with the apostles, he stood on a level place with a large number of his disciples. A large crowd of people was there from all over Judea and from Jerusalem and from the coast cities of Tyre and Sidon; <sup>18</sup>they had come to hear him and to be healed of their diseases. Those who were troubled by evil spirits also came and were healed. <sup>19</sup>All the people tried to touch him, for power was going out from him and healing them all.

### HAPPINESS AND SORROW

<sup>20</sup>Jesus looked at his disciples and said,

"Happy are you poor; the Kingdom of God is yours! [21]"Happy are you who are hungry now; you will be filled! "Happy are you who weep now; you will laugh!

[22]"Happy are you when people hate you, reject you, insult you, and say that you are evil, all because of the Son of Man! [23]Be glad when that happens and dance for joy, because a great reward is kept for you in heaven. For their ancestors did the very same things to the prophets.

[24]"But how terrible for you who are rich now; you have had your easy life! [25]"How terrible for you who are full now; you will go hungry! "How terrible for you who laugh now; you will mourn and weep!

[26]"How terrible when all people speak well of you; their ancestors said the very same things about the false prophets.

## LOVE FOR ENEMIES

[27]"But I tell you who hear me: Love your enemies, do good to those who hate you, [28]bless those who curse you, and pray for those who mistreat you. [29]If anyone hits you on one cheek, let him hit the other one too; if someone takes your coat, let him have your shirt as well. [30]Give to everyone who asks you for something, and when someone takes what is yours, do not ask for it back. [31]Do for others just what you want them to do for you.

[32]"If you love only the people who love you, why should you receive a blessing? Even sinners love those who love them! [33]And if you do good only to those who do good to you, why should you receive a blessing? Even sinners do that! [34]And if you lend only to those from whom you hope to get it back, why should you receive a blessing? Even sinners lend to sinners, to get back the same amount! [35]No! Love your enemies and do good to them; lend and expect nothing back. You will then have a great reward, and you will be children of the Most High God. For he is good to the ungrateful and the wicked. [36]Be merciful just as your Father is merciful.

## JUDGING OTHERS

[37]"Do not judge others, and God will not judge you; do not condemn others, and God will not condemn you; forgive others, and God will forgive you. [38]Give to others, and God will give to you. Indeed, you will receive a full measure, a generous helping, poured into your hands–all that you can hold. The measure you use for others is the one that God will use for you."

[39]And Jesus told them this parable: "One blind man cannot lead another one; if he does, both will fall into a ditch. [40]No pupils are greater than their teacher; but all pupils, when they have completed their training, will be like their teacher.

[41]"Why do you look at the speck in your brother's eye, but pay no attention to the log in your own eye? [42]How can you say to your brother, 'Please, brother, let me take that speck out of your eye,' yet cannot even see the log in your own eye? You hypocrite! First take the log out of your own eye, and then you will be able to see clearly to take the speck out of your brother's eye.

## A TREE AND ITS FRUIT

[43]"A healthy tree does not bear bad fruit, nor does a poor tree bear good fruit. [44]Every tree is known by the fruit it bears; you do not pick figs from thorn bushes or gather grapes from bramble bushes. [45]A good person brings good out of the treasure of good things in his heart; a bad person brings bad out of his treasure of bad things. For the mouth speaks what the heart is full of.

## THE TWO HOUSE BUILDERS

46"Why do you call me, 'Lord, Lord,' and yet don't do what I tell you? 47Anyone who comes to me and listens to my words and obeys them–I will show you what he is like. 48He is like a man who, in building his house, dug deep and laid the foundation on rock. The river flooded over and hit that house but could not shake it, because it was well built. 49But anyone who hears my words and does not obey them is like a man who built his house without laying a foundation; when the flood hit that house it fell at once–and what a terrible crash that was!"

## JESUS HEALS
## A ROMAN OFFICER'S SERVANT

7 When Jesus had finished saying all these things to the people, he went to Capernaum. 2A Roman officer there had a servant who was very dear to him; the man was sick and about to die. 3When the officer heard about Jesus, he sent some Jewish elders to ask him to come and heal his servant. 4They came to Jesus and begged him earnestly, "This man really deserves your help. 5He loves our people and he himself built a synagogue for us."

6So Jesus went with them. He was not far from the house when the officer sent friends to tell him, "Sir, don't trouble yourself. I do not deserve to have you come into my house, 7neither do I consider myself worthy to come to you in person. Just give the order, and my servant will get well. 8I, too, am a man placed under the authority of superior officers, and I have soldiers under me. I order this one, 'Go!' and he goes; I order that one, 'Come!' and he comes; and I order my slave, 'Do this!' and he does it."

9Jesus was surprised when he heard this; he turned around and said to the crowd following him, "I tell you, I have never found faith like this, not even in Israel!"

10The messengers went back to the officer's house and found his servant well.

## JESUS RAISES A WIDOW'S SON

11Soon afterward Jesus went to a town named Nain, accompanied by his disciples and a large crowd. 12Just as he arrived at the gate of the town, a funeral procession was coming out. The dead man was the only son of a woman who was a widow, and a large crowd from the town was with her. 13When the Lord saw her, his heart was filled with pity for her, and he said to her, "Don't cry." 14Then he walked over and touched the coffin, and the men carrying it stopped. Jesus said, "Young man! Get up, I tell you!" 15The dead man sat up and began to talk, and Jesus gave him back to his mother.

16They all were filled with fear and praised God. "A great prophet has appeared among us!" they said; "God has come to save his people!"

17This news about Jesus went out through all the country and the surrounding territory.

## THE MESSENGERS
## FROM JOHN THE BAPTIST

18When John's disciples told him about all these things, he called two of them 19and sent them to the Lord to ask him, "Are you the one John said was going to come, or should we expect someone else?"

20When they came to Jesus, they said, "John the Baptist sent us to ask if you are the one he said was going to come, or should we expect someone else?"

21At that very time Jesus healed many people from their sicknesses, diseases, and evil spirits, and gave sight to many blind people. 22He answered John's messengers, "Go back and tell John what you have seen and heard: the blind can see, the lame can walk, those who suffer from dreaded skin diseases are made clean, the deaf can hear, the dead are raised to life, and the Good News is preached to the poor. [23]How happy are those who have no doubts about me!"

[24]After John's messengers had left, Jesus began to speak about him to the crowds: "When you went out to John in the desert, what did you expect to see? A blade of grass bending in the wind? [25]What did you go out to see? A man dressed up in fancy clothes? People who dress like that and live in luxury are found in palaces! [26]Tell me, what did you go out to see? A prophet? Yes indeed, but you saw much more than a prophet. [27]For John is the one of whom the scripture says: 'God said, I will send my messenger ahead of you to open the way for you.' [28]I tell you," Jesus added, "John is greater than anyone who has ever lived. But the one who is least in the Kingdom of God is greater than John."

[29]All the people heard him; they and especially the tax collectors were the ones who had obeyed God's righteous demands and had been baptized by John. [30]But the Pharisees and the teachers of the Law rejected God's purpose for themselves and refused to be baptized by John.

[31]Jesus continued, "Now to what can I compare the people of this day? What are they like? [32]They are like children sitting in the marketplace. One group shouts to the other, 'We played wedding music for you, but you wouldn't dance! We sang funeral songs, but you wouldn't cry!' [33]John the Baptist came, and he fasted and drank no wine, and you said, 'He has a demon in him!' [34]The Son of Man came, and he ate and drank, and you said, 'Look at this man! He is a glutton and wine drinker, a friend of tax collectors and other outcasts!' [35]God's wisdom, however, is shown to be true by all who accept it."

## JESUS AT THE HOME OF SIMON THE PHARISEE

[36]A Pharisee invited Jesus to have dinner with him, and Jesus went to his house and sat down to eat. [37]In that town was a woman who lived a sinful life. She heard that Jesus was eating in the Pharisee's house, so she brought an alabaster jar full of perfume [38]and stood behind Jesus, by his feet, crying and wetting his feet with her tears. Then she dried his feet with her hair, kissed them, and poured the perfume on them. [39]When the Pharisee saw this, he said to himself, "If this man really were a prophet, he would know who this woman is who is touching him; he would know what kind of sinful life she lives!"

[40]Jesus spoke up and said to him, "Simon, I have something to tell you."

"Yes, Teacher," he said, "tell me."

[41]"There were two men who owed money to a moneylender," Jesus began. "One owed him five hundred silver coins, and the other owed him fifty. [42]Neither of them could pay him back, so he canceled the debts of both. Which one, then, will love him more?"

[43]"I suppose," answered Simon, "that it would be the one who was forgiven more."

"You are right," said Jesus. [44]Then he turned to the woman and said to Simon, "Do you see this woman? I came into your home, and you gave me no water for my feet, but she has washed my feet with her tears and dried them with her hair. [45]You did not welcome me with a kiss, but she has not stopped kissing my feet since I came. [46]You provided no olive oil for my head, but she has covered my feet with perfume. ⁴⁷I tell you, then, the great love she has shown proves that her many sins have been forgiven. But whoever has been forgiven little shows only a little love."

⁴⁸Then Jesus said to the woman, "Your sins are forgiven."

⁴⁹The others sitting at the table began to say to themselves, "Who is this, who even forgives sins?"

⁵⁰But Jesus said to the woman, "Your faith has saved you; go in peace."

## WOMEN WHO ACCOMPANIED JESUS

8 Some time later Jesus traveled through towns and villages, preaching the Good News about the Kingdom of God. The twelve disciples went with him, ²and so did some women who had been healed of evil spirits and diseases: Mary (who was called Magdalene), from whom seven demons had been driven out; ³Joanna, whose husband Chuza was an officer in Herod's court; and Susanna, and many other women who used their own resources to help Jesus and his disciples.

## THE PARABLE OF THE SOWER

⁴People kept coming to Jesus from one town after another; and when a great crowd gathered, Jesus told this parable:

⁵"Once there was a man who went out to sow grain. As he scattered the seed in the field, some of it fell along the path, where it was stepped on, and the birds ate it up. ⁶Some of it fell on rocky ground, and when the plants sprouted, they dried up because the soil had no moisture. ⁷Some of the seed fell among thorn bushes, which grew up with the plants and choked them. ⁸And some seeds fell in good soil; the plants grew and bore grain, one hundred grains each."

And Jesus concluded, "Listen, then, if you have ears!"

## THE PURPOSE OF THE PARABLES

⁹His disciples asked Jesus what this parable meant, ¹⁰and he answered, "The knowledge of the secrets of the Kingdom of God has been given to you, but to the rest it comes by means of parables, so that they may look but not see, and listen but not understand.

## JESUS EXPLAINS
## THE PARABLE OF THE SOWER

¹¹"This is what the parable means: the seed is the word of God. ¹²The seeds that fell along the path stand for those who hear; but the Devil comes and takes the message away from their hearts in order to keep them from believing and being saved. ¹³The seeds that fell on rocky ground stand for those who hear the message and receive it gladly. But it does not sink deep into them; they believe only for a while but when the time of testing comes, they fall away. ¹⁴The seeds that fell among thorn bushes stand for those who hear; but the worries and riches and pleasures of this life crowd in and choke them, and their fruit never ripens. ¹⁵The seeds that fell in good soil stand for those who hear the message and retain it in a good and obedient heart, and they persist until they bear fruit.

## A LAMP UNDER A BOWL

¹⁶"No one lights a lamp and covers it with a bowl or puts it under a bed. Instead, it is put on the lampstand, so that people will see the light as they come in.

¹⁷"Whatever is hidden away will be brought out into the open, and whatever is covered up will be found and brought to light.

¹⁸"Be careful, then, how you listen; because those who have something will be given more, but whoever has

nothing will have taken away from them even the little they think they have."

## JESUS' MOTHER AND BROTHERS

[19]Jesus' mother and brothers came to him, but were unable to join him because of the crowd. [20]Someone said to Jesus, "Your mother and brothers are standing outside and want to see you."

[21]Jesus said to them all, "My mother and brothers are those who hear the word of God and obey it."

## JESUS CALMS A STORM

[22]One day Jesus got into a boat with his disciples and said to them, "Let us go across to the other side of the lake." So they started out. [23]As they were sailing, Jesus fell asleep. Suddenly a strong wind blew down on the lake, and the boat began to fill with water, so that they were all in great danger. [24]The disciples went to Jesus and woke him up, saying, "Master, Master! We are about to die!"

Jesus got up and gave an order to the wind and to the stormy water; they quieted down, and there was a great calm. [25]Then he said to the disciples, "Where is your faith?"

But they were amazed and afraid, and said to one another, "Who is this man? He gives orders to the winds and waves, and they obey him!"

## JESUS HEALS A MAN WITH DEMONS

[26]Jesus and his disciples sailed on over to the territory of Gerasa, which is across the lake from Galilee. [27]As Jesus stepped ashore, he was met by a man from the town who had demons in him. For a long time this man had gone without clothes and would not stay at home, but spent his time in the burial caves. [28]When he saw Jesus, he gave a loud cry, threw himself down at his feet, and shouted, "Jesus, Son of the Most High God! What do you want with me? I beg you, don't punish me!" [29]He said this because Jesus had ordered the evil spirit to go out of him. Many times it had seized him, and even though he was kept a prisoner, his hands and feet tied with chains, he would break the chains and be driven by the demon out into the desert.

[30]Jesus asked him, "What is your name?"

"My name is 'Mob,' " he answered —because many demons had gone into him. [31]The demons begged Jesus not to send them into the abyss.

[32]There was a large herd of pigs near by, feeding on a hillside. So the demons begged Jesus to let them go into the pigs, and he let them. [33]They went out of the man and into the pigs. The whole herd rushed down the side of the cliff into the lake and was drowned.

[34]The men who had been taking care of the pigs saw what happened, so they ran off and spread the news in the town and among the farms. [35]People went out to see what had happened, and when they came to Jesus, they found the man from whom the demons had gone out sitting at the feet of Jesus, clothed and in his right mind; and they were all afraid. [36]Those who had seen it told the people how the man had been cured. [37]Then all the people from that territory asked Jesus to go away, because they were terribly afraid. So Jesus got into the boat and left. [38]The man from whom the demons had gone out begged Jesus, "Let me go with you."

But Jesus sent him away, saying, [39]"Go back home and tell what God has done for you."

The man went through the town, telling what Jesus had done for him.

## JAIRUS' DAUGHTER AND THE WOMAN WHO TOUCHED JESUS' CLOAK

[40]When Jesus returned to the other side of the lake, the people welcomed him, because they had all been waiting for him. [41]Then a man named Jairus arrived; he was an official in the local synagogue. He threw himself down at Jesus' feet and begged him to go to his home, [42]because his only daughter, who was twelve years old, was dying.

As Jesus went along, the people were crowding him from every side. [43]Among them was a woman who had suffered from severe bleeding for twelve years; she had spent all she had on doctors, but no one had been able to cure her. [44]She came up in the crowd behind Jesus and touched the edge of his cloak, and her bleeding stopped at once. [45]Jesus asked, "Who touched me?"

Everyone denied it, and Peter said, "Master, the people are all around you and crowding in on you."

[46]But Jesus said, "Someone touched me, for I knew it when power went out of me." [47]The woman saw that she had been found out, so she came trembling and threw herself at Jesus' feet. There in front of everybody, she told him why she had touched him and how she had been healed at once. [48]Jesus said to her, "My daughter, your faith has made you well. Go in peace."

[49]While Jesus was saying this, a messenger came from the official's house. "Your daughter has died," he told Jairus; "don't bother the Teacher any longer."

[50]But Jesus heard it and said to Jairus, "Don't be afraid; only believe, and she will be well."

[51]When he arrived at the house, he would not let anyone go in with him except Peter, John, and James, and the child's father and mother. [52]Everyone there was crying and mourning for the child. Jesus said, "Don't cry; the child is not dead—she is only sleeping!"

[53]They all made fun of him, because they knew that she was dead. [54]But Jesus took her by the hand and called out, "Get up, child!" [55]Her life returned, and she got up at once, and Jesus ordered them to give her something to eat. [56]Her parents were astounded, but Jesus commanded them not to tell anyone what had happened.

## JESUS SENDS OUT THE TWELVE DISCIPLES

9 Jesus called the twelve disciples together and gave them power and authority to drive out all demons and to cure diseases. [2]Then he sent them out to preach the Kingdom of God and to heal the sick, [3]after saying to them, "Take nothing with you for the trip: no walking stick, no beggar's bag, no food, no money, not even an extra shirt. [4]Wherever you are welcomed, stay in the same house until you leave that town; [5]wherever people don't welcome you, leave that town and shake the dust off your feet as a warning to them."

[6]The disciples left and traveled through all the villages, preaching the Good News and healing people everywhere.

## HEROD'S CONFUSION

[7]When Herod, the ruler of Galilee, heard about all the things that were happening, he was very confused, because some people were saying that John the Baptist had come back to life. [8]Others were saying that Elijah had appeared, and still others that one of the prophets of long ago had come back to life. [9]Herod said, "I had John's head cut off; but who is this man I hear these things about?" And he kept trying to see Jesus.

## JESUS FEEDS FIVE THOUSAND

[10]The apostles came back and told Jesus everything they had done. He took them with him, and they went off by themselves to a town named Bethsaida. [11]When the crowds heard about it, they followed him. He welcomed them, spoke to them about the Kingdom of God, and healed those who needed it.

[12]When the sun was beginning to set, the twelve disciples came to him and said, "Send the people away so that they can go to the villages and farms around here and find food and lodging, because this is a lonely place."

[13]But Jesus said to them, "You yourselves give them something to eat."

They answered, "All we have are five loaves and two fish. Do you want us to go and buy food for this whole crowd?" [14](There were about five thousand men there.)

Jesus said to his disciples, "Make the people sit down in groups of about fifty each."

[15]After the disciples had done so, [16]Jesus took the five loaves and two fish, looked up to heaven, thanked God for them, broke them, and gave them to the disciples to distribute to the people. [17]They all ate and had enough, and the disciples took up twelve baskets of what was left over.

## PETER'S DECLARATION ABOUT JESUS

[18] One day when Jesus was praying alone, the disciples came to him. "Who do the crowds say I am?" he asked them.

[19]"Some say that you are John the Baptist," they answered. "Others say that you are Elijah, while others say that one of the prophets of long ago has come back to life."

[20]"What about you?" he asked them. "Who do you say I am?"

Peter answered, "You are God's Messiah."

## JESUS SPEAKS ABOUT HIS SUFFERING AND DEATH

[21]Then Jesus gave them strict orders not to tell this to anyone. [22]He also told them, "The Son of Man must suffer much and be rejected by the elders, the chief priests, and the teachers of the Law. He will be put to death, but three days later he will be raised to life."

[23]And he said to them all, "If you want to come with me, you must forget yourself, take up your cross every day, and follow me. [24]For if you want to save your own life, you will lose it, but if you lose your life for my sake, you will save it. [25]Will you gain anything if you win the whole world but are yourself lost or defeated? Of course not! [26]If you are ashamed of me and of my teaching, then the Son of Man will be ashamed of you when he comes in his glory and in the glory of the Father and of the holy angels. [27]I assure you that there are some here who will not die until they have seen the Kingdom of God."

## THE TRANSFIGURATION

[28]About a week after he had said these things, Jesus took Peter, John, and James with him and went up a hill to pray. [29]While he was praying, his face changed its appearance, and his clothes became dazzling white. [30]Suddenly two men were there talking with him. They were Moses and Elijah, [31]who appeared in heavenly glory and talked with Jesus about the way in which he would soon fulfill God's purpose by dying in Jerusalem. [32]Peter and his companions were sound asleep, but they woke up and saw Jesus' glory and the two men who were standing with him. [33]As the men were leaving Jesus, Peter said to him, "Master, how good it is that we are

here! We will make three tents, one for you, one for Moses, and one for Elijah." (He did not really know what he was saying.)

[34]While he was still speaking, a cloud appeared and covered them with its shadow; and the disciples were afraid as the cloud came over them. [35]A voice said from the cloud, "This is my Son, whom I have chosen –listen to him!"

[36]When the voice stopped, there was Jesus all alone. The disciples kept quiet about all this and told no one at that time anything they had seen.

### JESUS HEALS A BOY WITH AN EVIL SPIRIT

[37]The next day Jesus and the three disciples went down from the hill, and a large crowd met Jesus. [38]A man shouted from the crowd, "Teacher! I beg you, look at my son–my only son! [39]A spirit attacks him with a sudden shout and throws him into a fit, so that he foams at the mouth; it keeps on hurting him and will hardly let him go! [40]I begged your disciples to drive it out, but they couldn't."

[41]Jesus answered, "How unbelieving and wrong you people are! How long must I stay with you? How long do I have to put up with you?" Then he said to the man, "Bring your son here."

[42]As the boy was coming, the demon knocked him to the ground and threw him into a fit. Jesus gave a command to the evil spirit, healed the boy, and gave him back to his father. [43]All the people were amazed at the mighty power of God.

### JESUS SPEAKS AGAIN ABOUT HIS DEATH

The people were still marveling at everything Jesus was doing, when he said to his disciples, [44]"Don't forget what I am about to tell you! The Son of Man is going to be handed over to the power of human beings." [45]But the disciples did not know what this meant. It had been hidden from them so that they could not understand it, and they were afraid to ask him about the matter.

### WHO IS THE GREATEST?

[46]An argument broke out among the disciples as to which one of them was the greatest. [47]Jesus knew what they were thinking, so he took a child, stood him by his side, [48]and said to them, "Whoever welcomes this child in my name, welcomes me; and who-ever welcomes me, also welcomes the one who sent me. For the one who is least among you all is the greatest."

### WHOEVER IS NOT AGAINST YOU IS FOR YOU

[49]John spoke up, "Master, we saw a man driving out demons in your name, and we told him to stop, because he doesn't belong to our group."

[50]"Do not try to stop him," Jesus said to him and to the other disciples, "because whoever is not against you is for you."

### A SAMARITAN VILLAGE REFUSES TO RECEIVE JESUS

[51]As the time drew near when Jesus would be taken up to heaven, he made up his mind and set out on his way to Jerusalem. [52]He sent messengers ahead of him, who went into a village in Samaria to get everything ready for him. [53]But the people there would not receive him, because it was clear that he was on his way to Jerusalem. [54]When the disciples James and John saw this, they said, "Lord, do you want us to call fire down from heaven to destroy them?"

[55]Jesus turned and rebuked them. [56]Then Jesus and his disciples went on to another village.

## THE WOULD-BE FOLLOWERS OF JESUS

⁵⁷As they went on their way, a man said to Jesus, "I will follow you wherever you go."

⁵⁸Jesus said to him, "Foxes have holes, and birds have nests, but the Son of Man has no place to lie down and rest."

⁵⁹He said to another man, "Follow me."

But that man said, "Sir, first let me go back and bury my father."

⁶⁰Jesus answered, "Let the dead bury their own dead. You go and proclaim the Kingdom of God."

⁶¹Someone else said, "I will follow you, sir; but first let me go and say good-bye to my family."

⁶²Jesus said to him, "Anyone who starts to plow and then keeps looking back is of no use for the Kingdom of God."

## JESUS SENDS OUT THE SEVENTY-TWO

10 After this the Lord chose another seventy-two men and sent them out two by two, to go ahead of him to every town and place where he himself was about to go. ²He said to them, "There is a large harvest, but few workers to gather it in. Pray to the owner of the harvest that he will send out workers to gather in his harvest. ³Go! I am sending you like lambs among wolves. ⁴Don't take a purse or a beggar's bag or shoes; don't stop to greet anyone on the road. ⁵Whenever you go into a house, first say, 'Peace be with this house.' ⁶If someone who is peace-loving lives there, let your greeting of peace remain on that person; if not, take back your greeting of peace. ⁷Stay in that same house, eating and drinking whatever they offer you, for workers should be given their pay. Don't move around from one house to another. ⁸Whenever you go into a town and are made welcome, eat what is set before you, ⁹heal the sick in that town, and say to the people there, 'The Kingdom of God has come near you.' ¹⁰But whenever you go into a town and are not welcomed, go out in the streets and say, ¹¹'Even the dust from your town that sticks to our feet we wipe off against you. But remember that the Kingdom of God has come near you!' ¹²I assure you that on the Judgment Day God will show more mercy to Sodom than to that town!

## THE UNBELIEVING TOWNS

¹³"How terrible it will be for you, Chorazin! How terrible for you too, Bethsaida! If the miracles which were performed in you had been performed in Tyre and Sidon, the people there would have long ago sat down, put on sackcloth, and sprinkled ashes on themselves, to show that they had turned from their sins! ¹⁴God will show more mercy on the Judgment Day to Tyre and Sidon than to you. ¹⁵And as for you, Capernaum! Did you want to lift yourself up to heaven? You will be thrown down to hell!"

¹⁶Jesus said to his disciples, "Whoever listens to you listens to me; whoever rejects you rejects me; and whoever rejects me rejects the one who sent me."

## THE RETURN OF THE SEVENTY-TWO

¹⁷The seventy-two men came back in great joy. "Lord," they said, "even the demons obeyed us when we gave them a command in your name!"

¹⁸ Jesus answered them, "I saw Satan fall like lightning from heaven. ¹⁹Listen! I have given you authority, so that you can walk on snakes and scorpions and overcome all the power of the Enemy, and nothing will hurt you. ²⁰But don't be glad because the evil spirits obey you; rather be glad

because your names are written in heaven."

## JESUS REJOICES

²¹At that time Jesus was filled with joy by the Holy Spirit and said, "Father, Lord of heaven and earth! I thank you because you have shown to the unlearned what you have hidden from the wise and learned. Yes, Father, this was how you were pleased to have it happen.

²²"My Father has given me all things. No one knows who the Son is except the Father, and no one knows who the Father is except the Son and those to whom the Son chooses to reveal him."

²³Then Jesus turned to the disciples and said to them privately, "How fortunate you are to see the things you see! ²⁴I tell you that many prophets and kings wanted to see what you see, but they could not, and to hear what you hear, but they did not."

## THE PARABLE
## OF THE GOOD SAMARITAN

²⁵A teacher of the Law came up and tried to trap Jesus. "Teacher," he asked, "what must I do to receive eternal life?"

²⁶Jesus answered him, "What do the Scriptures say? How do you interpret them?"

²⁷The man answered, " 'Love the Lord your God with all your heart, with all your soul, with all your strength, and with all your mind'; and 'Love your neighbor as you love yourself.' "

²⁸"You are right," Jesus replied; "do this and you will live."

²⁹But the teacher of the Law wanted to justify himself, so he asked Jesus, "Who is my neighbor?"

³⁰Jesus answered, "There was once a man who was going down from Jerusalem to Jericho when robbers attacked him, stripped him, and beat him up, leaving him half dead. ³¹It so happened that a priest was going down that road; but when he saw the man, he walked on by on the other side. ³²In the same way a Levite also came there, went over and looked at the man, and then walked on by on the other side. ³³But a Samaritan who was traveling that way came upon the man, and when he saw him, his heart was filled with pity. ³⁴He went over to him, poured oil and wine on his wounds and bandaged them; then he put the man on his own animal and took him to an inn, where he took care of him. ³⁵The next day he took out two silver coins and gave them to the innkeeper. 'Take care of him,' he told the innkeeper, 'and when I come back this way, I will pay you whatever else you spend on him.' "

³⁶And Jesus concluded, "In your opinion, which one of these three acted like a neighbor toward the man attacked by the robbers?"

³⁷The teacher of the Law answered, "The one who was kind to him."

Jesus replied, "You go, then, and do the same."

## JESUS VISITS MARTHA AND MARY

³⁸As Jesus and his disciples went on their way, he came to a village where a woman named Martha welcomed him in her home. ³⁹She had a sister named Mary, who sat down at the feet of the Lord and listened to his teaching. ⁴⁰Martha was upset over all the work she had to do, so she came and said, "Lord, don't you care that my sister has left me to do all the work by myself? Tell her to come and help me!"

⁴¹The Lord answered her, "Martha, Martha! You are worried and troubled over so many things, ⁴²but just one is needed. Mary has chosen the right

thing, and it will not be taken away from her."

## JESUS' TEACHING ON PRAYER

11 One day Jesus was praying in a certain place. When he had finished, one of his disciples said to him, "Lord, teach us to pray, just as John taught his disciples."

[2]Jesus said to them, "When you pray, say this:

'Father: may your holy name be honored; may your Kingdom come. [3]Give us day by day the food we need. [4]Forgive us our sins, for we forgive everyone who does us wrong. And do not bring us to hard testing.' "

[5]And Jesus said to his disciples, "Suppose one of you should go to a friend's house at midnight and say, 'Friend, let me borrow three loaves of bread. [6]A friend of mine who is on a trip has just come to my house, and I don't have any food for him!' [7]And suppose your friend should answer from inside, 'Don't bother me! The door is already locked, and my children and I are in bed. I can't get up and give you anything.' [8]Well, what then? I tell you that even if he will not get up and give you the bread because you are his friend, yet he will get up and give you everything you need because you are not ashamed to keep on asking. [9]And so I say to you: Ask, and you will receive; seek, and you will find; knock, and the door will be opened to you. [10]For those who ask will receive, and those who seek will find, and the door will be opened to anyone who knocks. [11]Would any of you who are fathers give your son a snake when he asks for fish? [12]Or would you give him a scorpion when he asks for an egg? [13]As bad as you are, you know how to give good things to your children. How much more, then, will the Father in heaven give the Holy Spirit to those who ask him!"

## JESUS AND BEELZEBUL

[14]Jesus was driving out a demon that could not talk; and when the demon went out, the man began to talk. The crowds were amazed, [15]but some of the people said, "It is Beelzebul, the chief of the demons, who gives him the power to drive them out."

[16]Others wanted to trap Jesus, so they asked him to perform a miracle to show that God approved of him. [17]But Jesus knew what they were thinking, so he said to them, "Any country that divides itself into groups which fight each other will not last very long; a family divided against itself falls apart. [18]So if Satan's kingdom has groups fighting each other, how can it last? You say that I drive out demons because Beelzebul gives me the power to do so. [19]If this is how I drive them out, how do your followers drive them out? Your own followers prove that you are wrong! [20]No, it is rather by means of God's power that I drive out demons, and this proves that the Kingdom of God has already come to you.

[21]"When a strong man, with all his weapons ready, guards his own house, all his belongings are safe. [22]But when a stronger man attacks him and defeats him, he carries away all the weapons the owner was depending on and divides up what he stole.

[23]"Anyone who is not for me is really against me; anyone who does not help me gather is really scattering.

## THE RETURN OF THE EVIL SPIRIT

[24]"When an evil spirit goes out of a person, it travels over dry country looking for a place to rest. If it can't find one, it says to itself, 'I will go back to my house.' [25]So it goes back and finds the house clean and all fixed up. [26]Then it goes out and brings seven other spirits even worse than itself, and they come and live there.

So when it is all over, that person is in worse shape than at the beginning."

## TRUE HAPPINESS

²⁷When Jesus had said this, a woman spoke up from the crowd and said to him, "How happy is the woman who bore you and nursed you!"

²⁸But Jesus answered, "Rather, how happy are those who hear the word of God and obey it!"

## THE DEMAND FOR A MIRACLE

²⁹As the people crowded around Jesus, he went on to say, "How evil are the people of this day! They ask for a miracle, but none will be given them except the miracle of Jonah. ³⁰In the same way that the prophet Jonah was a sign for the people of Nineveh, so the Son of Man will be a sign for the people of this day. ³¹On the Judgment Day the Queen of Sheba will stand up and accuse the people of today, because she traveled all the way from her country to listen to King Solomon's wise teaching; and there is something here, I tell you, greater than Solomon. ³²On the Judgment Day the people of Nineveh will stand up and accuse you, because they turned from their sins when they heard Jonah preach; and I assure you that there is something here greater than Jonah!

## THE LIGHT OF THE BODY

³³"No one lights a lamp and then hides it or puts it under a bowl; instead, it is put on the lampstand, so that people may see the light as they come in. ³⁴Your eyes are like a lamp for the body. When your eyes are sound, your whole body is full of light; but when your eyes are no good, your whole body will be in darkness. ³⁵Make certain, then, that the light in you is not darkness. ³⁶If your whole body is full of light, with no part of it in darkness, it will be bright all over,

as when a lamp shines on you with its brightness."

## JESUS ACCUSES THE PHARISEES AND THE TEACHERS OF THE LAW

³⁷When Jesus finished speaking, a Pharisee invited him to eat with him; so he went in and sat down to eat. ³⁸The Pharisee was surprised when he noticed that Jesus had not washed before eating. ³⁹So the Lord said to him, "Now then, you Pharisees clean the outside of your cup and plate, but inside you are full of violence and evil. ⁴⁰Fools! Did not God, who made the outside, also make the inside? ⁴¹But give what is in your cups and plates to the poor, and everything will be ritually clean for you.

⁴²"How terrible for you Pharisees! You give to God one tenth of the seasoning herbs, such as mint and rue and all the other herbs, but you neglect justice and love for God. These you should practice, without neglecting the others.

⁴³"How terrible for you Pharisees! You love the reserved seats in the synagogues and to be greeted with respect in the marketplaces. ⁴⁴How terrible for you! You are like unmarked graves which people walk on without knowing it."

⁴⁵One of the teachers of the Law said to him, "Teacher, when you say this, you insult us too!"

⁴⁶Jesus answered, "How terrible also for you teachers of the Law! You put onto people's backs loads which are hard to carry, but you yourselves will not stretch out a finger to help them carry those loads. ⁴⁷How terrible for you! You make fine tombs for the prophets–the very prophets your ancestors murdered. ⁴⁸You yourselves admit, then, that you approve of what your ancestors did; they murdered the prophets, and you build their tombs. ⁴⁹For this reason the Wisdom of God said, 'I will send them prophets and

messengers; they will kill some of them and persecute others.' ⁵⁰So the people of this time will be punished for the murder of all the prophets killed since the creation of the world, ⁵¹from the murder of Abel to the murder of Zechariah, who was killed between the altar and the Holy Place. Yes, I tell you, the people of this time will be punished for them all!

⁵²"How terrible for you teachers of the Law! You have kept the key that opens the door to the house of knowledge; you yourselves will not go in, and you stop those who are trying to go in!"

⁵³When Jesus left that place, the teachers of the Law and the Pharisees began to criticize him bitterly and ask him questions about many things, ⁵⁴trying to lay traps for him and catch him saying something wrong.

## A WARNING AGAINST HYPOCRISY

12 As thousands of people crowded together, so that they were stepping on each other, Jesus said first to his disciples, "Be on guard against the yeast of the Pharisees–I mean their hypocrisy. ²Whatever is covered up will be uncovered, and every secret will be made known. ³So then, whatever you have said in the dark will be heard in broad daylight, and whatever you have whispered in private in a closed room will be shouted from the housetops.

## WHOM TO FEAR

⁴"I tell you, my friends, do not be afraid of those who kill the body but cannot afterward do anything worse. ⁵I will show you whom to fear: fear God, who, after killing, has the authority to throw into hell. Believe me, he is the one you must fear!

⁶"Aren't five sparrows sold for two pennies? Yet not one sparrow is forgotten by God. ⁷Even the hairs of your head have all been counted. So do not

be afraid; you are worth much more than many sparrows!

## CONFESSING AND REJECTING CHRIST

⁸"I assure you that those who declare publicly that they belong to me, the Son of Man will do the same for them before the angels of God. ⁹But those who reject me publicly, the Son of Man will also reject them before the angels of God.

¹⁰"Whoever says a word against the Son of Man can be forgiven; but whoever says evil things against the Holy Spirit will not be forgiven.

¹¹"When they bring you to be tried in the synagogues or before governors or rulers, do not be worried about how you will defend yourself or what you will say. ¹²For the Holy Spirit will teach you at that time what you should say."

## THE PARABLE OF THE RICH FOOL

¹³A man in the crowd said to Jesus, "Teacher, tell my brother to divide with me the property our father left us."

¹⁴Jesus answered him, "Friend, who gave me the right to judge or to divide the property between you two?" ¹⁵And he went on to say to them all, "Watch out and guard yourselves from every kind of greed; because your true life is not made up of the things you own, no matter how rich you may be."

¹⁶Then Jesus told them this parable: "There was once a rich man who had land which bore good crops. ¹⁷He began to think to himself, 'I don't have a place to keep all my crops. What can I do? ¹⁸This is what I will do,' he told himself; 'I will tear down my barns and build bigger ones, where I will store the grain and all my other goods. ¹⁹Then I will say to myself, Lucky man! You have all the good things you need for many years. Take life easy, eat, drink, and enjoy

yourself!' [20]But God said to him, 'You fool! This very night you will have to give up your life; then who will get all these things you have kept for yourself?' "

[21]And Jesus concluded, "This is how it is with those who pile up riches for themselves but are not rich in God's sight."

### TRUST IN GOD

[22]Then Jesus said to the disciples, "And so I tell you not to worry about the food you need to stay alive or about the clothes you need for your body. [23]Life is much more important than food, and the body much more important than clothes. [24]Look at the crows: they don't plant seeds or gather a harvest; they don't have storage rooms or barns; God feeds them! You are worth so much more than birds! [25]Can any of you live a bit longer by worrying about it? [26]If you can't manage even such a small thing, why worry about the other things? [27]Look how the wild flowers grow: they don't work or make clothes for themselves. But I tell you that not even King Solomon with all his wealth had clothes as beautiful as one of these flowers. [28]It is God who clothes the wild grass–grass that is here today and gone tomorrow, burned up in the oven. Won't he be all the more sure to clothe you? What little faith you have!

[29]"So don't be all upset, always concerned about what you will eat and drink. [30](For the pagans of this world are always concerned about all these things.) Your Father knows that you need these things. [31]Instead, be concerned with his Kingdom, and he will provide you with these things.

### RICHES IN HEAVEN

[32]"Do not be afraid, little flock, for your Father is pleased to give you the Kingdom. [33]Sell all your belongings and give the money to the poor. Provide for yourselves purses that don't wear out, and save your riches in heaven, where they will never decrease, because no thief can get to them, and no moth can destroy them. [34]For your heart will always be where your riches are.

### WATCHFUL SERVANTS

[35]"Be ready for whatever comes, dressed for action and with your lamps lit, [36]like servants who are waiting for their master to come back from a wedding feast. When he comes and knocks, they will open the door for him at once. [37]How happy are those servants whose master finds them awake and ready when he returns! I tell you, he will take off his coat, have them sit down, and will wait on them. [38]How happy they are if he finds them ready, even if he should come at midnight or even later! [39]And you can be sure that if the owner of a house knew the time when the thief would come, he would not let the thief break into his house. [40]And you, too, must be ready, because the Son of Man will come at an hour when you are not expecting him."

### THE FAITHFUL
### OR THE UNFAITHFUL SERVANT

[41]Peter said, "Lord, does this parable apply to us, or do you mean it for everyone?"

[42]The Lord answered, "Who, then, is the faithful and wise servant? He is the one that his master will put in charge, to run the household and give the other servants their share of the food at the proper time. [43]How happy that servant is if his master finds him doing this when he comes home! [44]Indeed, I tell you, the master will put that servant in charge of all his property. [45]But if that servant says to himself that his master is taking a long time to come back and if he begins to beat the other servants, both the men and the women, and eats

and drinks and gets drunk, ⁴⁶then the master will come back one day when the servant does not expect him and at a time he does not know. The master will cut him in pieces and make him share the fate of the disobedient.

⁴⁷"The servant who knows what his master wants him to do, but does not get himself ready and do it, will be punished with a heavy whipping. ⁴⁸But the servant who does not know what his master wants, and yet does something for which he deserves a whipping, will be punished with a light whipping. Much is required from the person to whom much is given; much more is required from the person to whom much more is given.

## JESUS THE CAUSE OF DIVISION

⁴⁹"I came to set the earth on fire, and how I wish it were already kindled! ⁵⁰I have a baptism to receive, and how distressed I am until it is over! ⁵¹Do you suppose that I came to bring peace to the world? No, not peace, but division. ⁵²From now on a family of five will be divided, three against two and two against three. ⁵³Fathers will be against their sons, and sons against their fathers; mothers will be against their daughters, and daughters against their mothers; mothers-in-law will be against their daughters-in-law, and daughters-in-law against their mothers-in-law."

## UNDERSTANDING THE TIME

⁵⁴Jesus said also to the people, "When you see a cloud coming up in the west, at once you say that it is going to rain–and it does. ⁵⁵And when you feel the south wind blowing, you say that it is going to get hot–and it does. ⁵⁶Hypocrites! You can look at the earth and the sky and predict the weather; why, then, don't you know the meaning of this present time?

## SETTLE WITH YOUR OPPONENT

⁵⁷"Why do you not judge for yourselves the right thing to do? ⁵⁸If someone brings a lawsuit against you and takes you to court, do your best to settle the dispute before you get to court. If you don't, you will be dragged before the judge, who will hand you over to the police, and you will be put in jail. ⁵⁹There you will stay, I tell you, until you pay the last penny of your fine."

## TURN FROM YOUR SINS OR DIE

13 At that time some people were there who told Jesus about the Galileans whom Pilate had killed while they were offering sacrifices to God. ²Jesus answered them, "Because those Galileans were killed in that way, do you think it proves that they were worse sinners than all other Galileans? ³No indeed! And I tell you that if you do not turn from your sins, you will all die as they did. ⁴What about those eighteen people in Siloam who were killed when the tower fell on them? Do you suppose this proves that they were worse than all the other people living in Jerusalem? ⁵No indeed! And I tell you that if you do not turn from your sins, you will all die as they did."

## THE PARABLE
## OF THE UNFRUITFUL FIG TREE

⁶Then Jesus told them this parable: "There was once a man who had a fig tree growing in his vineyard. He went looking for figs on it but found none. ⁷So he said to his gardener, 'Look, for three years I have been coming here looking for figs on this fig tree, and I haven't found any. Cut it down! Why should it go on using up the soil?' ⁸But the gardener answered, 'Leave it alone, sir, just one more year; I will dig around it and put in some fertilizer. ⁹Then if the tree bears figs next year, so

much the better; if not, then you can have it cut down.' "

## JESUS HEALS A CRIPPLED WOMAN ON THE SABBATH

[10]One Sabbath Jesus was teaching in a synagogue. [11]A woman there had an evil spirit that had kept her sick for eighteen years; she was bent over and could not straighten up at all. [12]When Jesus saw her, he called out to her, "Woman, you are free from your sickness!" [13]He placed his hands on her, and at once she straightened herself up and praised God.

[14]The official of the synagogue was angry that Jesus had healed on the Sabbath, so he spoke up and said to the people, "There are six days in which we should work; so come during those days and be healed, but not on the Sabbath!"

[15]The Lord answered him, "You hypocrites! Any one of you would untie your ox or your donkey from the stall and take it out to give it water on the Sabbath. [16]Now here is this descendant of Abraham whom Satan has kept in bonds for eighteen years; should she not be released on the Sabbath?" [17]His answer made his enemies ashamed of themselves, while the people rejoiced over all the wonderful things that he did.

## THE PARABLE OF THE MUSTARD SEED

[18]Jesus asked, "What is the Kingdom of God like? What shall I compare it with? [19]It is like this. A man takes a mustard seed and plants it in his field. The plant grows and becomes a tree, and the birds make their nests in its branches."

## THE PARABLE OF THE YEAST

[20]Again Jesus asked, "What shall I compare the Kingdom of God with? [21]It is like this. A woman takes some yeast and mixes it with a bushel of flour until the whole batch of dough rises."

## THE NARROW DOOR

[22]Jesus went through towns and villages, teaching the people and making his way toward Jerusalem. [23]Someone asked him, "Sir, will just a few people be saved?"

Jesus answered them, [24]"Do your best to go in through the narrow door; because many people will surely try to go in but will not be able. [25]The master of the house will get up and close the door; then when you stand outside and begin to knock on the door and say, 'Open the door for us, sir!' he will answer you, 'I don't know where you come from!' [26]Then you will answer, 'We ate and drank with you; you taught in our town!' [27]But he will say again, 'I don't know where you come from. Get away from me, all you wicked people!' [28]How you will cry and gnash your teeth when you see Abraham, Isaac, and Jacob, and all the prophets in the Kingdom of God, while you are thrown out! [29]People will come from the east and the west, from the north and the south, and sit down at the feast in the Kingdom of God. [30]Then those who are now last will be first, and those who are now first will be last."

## JESUS' LOVE FOR JERUSALEM

[31]At that same time some Pharisees came to Jesus and said to him, "You must get out of here and go somewhere else, because Herod wants to kill you."

[32]Jesus answered them, "Go and tell that fox: 'I am driving out demons and performing cures today and tomorrow, and on the third day I shall finish my work.' [33]Yet I must be on my way today, tomorrow, and the next day; it is not right for a prophet to be killed anywhere except in Jerusalem.

34"Jerusalem, Jerusalem! You kill the prophets, you stone the messengers God has sent you! How many times I wanted to put my arms around all your people, just as a hen gathers her chicks under her wings, but you would not let me! 35And so your Temple will be abandoned. I assure you that you will not see me until the time comes when you say, 'God bless him who comes in the name of the Lord.' "

### JESUS HEALS A SICK MAN

14 One Sabbath Jesus went to eat a meal at the home of one of the leading Pharisees; and people were watching Jesus closely. 2A man whose legs and arms were swollen came to Jesus, 3and Jesus spoke up and asked the teachers of the Law and the Pharisees, "Does our Law allow healing on the Sabbath or not?"

4But they would not say a thing. Jesus took the man, healed him, and sent him away. 5Then he said to them, "If any one of you had a child or an ox that happened to fall in a well on a Sabbath, would you not pull it out at once on the Sabbath itself?"

6But they were not able to answer him about this.

### HUMILITY AND HOSPITALITY

7Jesus noticed how some of the guests were choosing the best places, so he told this parable to all of them: 8"When someone invites you to a wedding feast, do not sit down in the best place. It could happen that someone more important than you has been invited, 9and your host, who invited both of you, would have to come and say to you, 'Let him have this place.' Then you would be embarrassed and have to sit in the lowest place. 10Instead, when you are invited, go and sit in the lowest place, so that your host will come to you and say, 'Come on up, my friend, to a better place.'

This will bring you honor in the presence of all the other guests. 11For those who make themselves great will be humbled, and those who humble themselves will be made great."

12Then Jesus said to his host, "When you give a lunch or a dinner, do not invite your friends or your brothers or your relatives or your rich neighbors–for they will invite you back, and in this way you will be paid for what you did. 13When you give a feast, invite the poor, the crippled, the lame, and the blind; 14and you will be blessed, because they are not able to pay you back. God will repay you on the day the good people rise from death."

### THE PARABLE OF THE GREAT FEAST

15When one of the guests sitting at the table heard this, he said to Jesus, "How happy are those who will sit down at the feast in the Kingdom of God!"

16Jesus said to him, "There was once a man who was giving a great feast to which he invited many people. 17When it was time for the feast, he sent his servant to tell his guests, 'Come, everything is ready!' 18But they all began, one after another, to make excuses. The first one told the servant, 'I have bought a field and must go and look at it; please accept my apologies.' 19Another one said, 'I have bought five pairs of oxen and am on my way to try them out; please accept my apologies.' 20Another one said, 'I have just gotten married, and for that reason I cannot come.' 21The servant went back and told all this to his master. The master was furious and said to his servant, 'Hurry out to the streets and alleys of the town, and bring back the poor, the crippled, the blind, and the lame.' 22Soon the servant said, 'Your order has been carried out, sir, but there is room for more.' 23So the master said to the servant,

'Go out to the country roads and lanes and make people come in, so that my house will be full. [24]I tell you all that none of those who were invited will taste my dinner!' "

### THE COST OF BEING A DISCIPLE

[25]Once when large crowds of people were going along with Jesus, he turned and said to them, [26]"Those who come to me cannot be my disciples unless they love me more than they love father and mother, wife and children, brothers and sisters, and themselves as well. [27]Those who do not carry their own cross and come after me cannot be my disciples. [28]If one of you is planning to build a tower, you sit down first and figure out what it will cost, to see if you have enough money to finish the job. [29]If you don't, you will not be able to finish the tower after laying the foundation; and all who see what happened will make fun of you. [30]'You began to build but can't finish the job!' they will say. [31]If a king goes out with ten thousand men to fight another king who comes against him with twenty thousand men, he will sit down first and decide if he is strong enough to face that other king. [32]If he isn't, he will send messengers to meet the other king to ask for terms of peace while he is still a long way off. [33]In the same way," concluded Jesus, "none of you can be my disciple unless you give up everything you have.

### WORTHLESS SALT

[34]"Salt is good, but if it loses its saltiness, there is no way to make it salty again. [35]It is no good for the soil or for the manure pile; it is thrown away. Listen, then, if you have ears!"

### THE LOST SHEEP

**15** One day when many tax collectors and other outcasts came to listen to Jesus, [2]the Pharisees and the teachers of the Law started grumbling, "This man welcomes outcasts and even eats with them!" [3]So Jesus told them this parable:

[4]"Suppose one of you has a hundred sheep and loses one of them–what do you do? You leave the other ninety-nine sheep in the pasture and go looking for the one that got lost until you find it. [5]When you find it, you are so happy that you put it on your shoulders [6]and carry it back home. Then you call your friends and neighbors together and say to them, 'I am so happy I found my lost sheep. Let us celebrate!' [7]In the same way, I tell you, there will be more joy in heaven over one sinner who repents than over ninety-nine respectable people who do not need to repent.

### THE LOST COIN

[8]"Or suppose a woman who has ten silver coins loses one of them–what does she do? She lights a lamp, sweeps her house, and looks carefully everywhere until she finds it. [9]When she finds it, she calls her friends and neighbors together, and says to them, 'I am so happy I found the coin I lost. Let us celebrate!' [10]In the same way, I tell you, the angels of God rejoice over one sinner who repents."

### THE LOST SON

[11]Jesus went on to say, "There was once a man who had two sons. [12]The younger one said to him, 'Father, give me my share of the property now.' So the man divided his property between his two sons. [13]After a few days the younger son sold his part of the property and left home with the money. He went to a country far away, where he wasted his money in reckless living. [14]He spent everything he had. Then a severe famine spread over that country, and he was left without a thing. [15]So he went to work for one of the citizens of that country, who sent him

out to his farm to take care of the pigs. [16]He wished he could fill himself with the bean pods the pigs ate, but no one gave him anything to eat. [17]At last he came to his senses and said, 'All my father's hired workers have more than they can eat, and here I am about to starve! [18]I will get up and go to my father and say, Father, I have sinned against God and against you. [19]I am no longer fit to be called your son; treat me as one of your hired workers.' [20]So he got up and started back to his father.

"He was still a long way from home when his father saw him; his heart was filled with pity, and he ran, threw his arms around him, and kissed him. [21]'Father,' the son said, 'I have sinned against God and against you. I am no longer fit to be called your son.' [22]But the father called to his servants. 'Hurry!' he said. 'Bring the best robe and put it on him. Put a ring on his finger and shoes on his feet. [23]Then go and get the prize calf and kill it, and let us celebrate with a feast! [24]For this son of mine was dead, but now he is alive; he was lost, but now he has been found.' And so the feasting began.

[25]"In the meantime the older son was out in the field. On his way back, when he came close to the house, he heard the music and dancing. [26]So he called one of the servants and asked him, 'What's going on?' [27]'Your brother has come back home,' the servant answered, 'and your father has killed the prize calf, because he got him back safe and sound.' [28]The older brother was so angry that he would not go into the house; so his father came out and begged him to come in. [29]But he spoke back to his father, 'Look, all these years I have worked for you like a slave, and I have never disobeyed your orders. What have you given me? Not even a goat for me to have a feast with my friends! [30]But this son of yours wasted all your prop-

erty on prostitutes, and when he comes back home, you kill the prize calf for him!' [31]'My son,' the father answered, 'you are always here with me, and everything I have is yours. [32]But we had to celebrate and be happy, because your brother was dead, but now he is alive; he was lost, but now he has been found.' "

## THE SHREWD MANAGER

**16** Jesus said to his disciples, "There was once a rich man who had a servant who managed his property. The rich man was told that the manager was wasting his master's money, [2]so he called him in and said, 'What is this I hear about you? Turn in a complete account of your handling of my property, because you cannot be my manager any longer.' [3]The servant said to himself, 'My master is going to dismiss me from my job. What shall I do? I am not strong enough to dig ditches, and I am ashamed to beg. [4]Now I know what I will do! Then when my job is gone, I shall have friends who will welcome me in their homes.' [5]So he called in all the people who were in debt to his master. He asked the first one, 'How much do you owe my master?' [6]'One hundred barrels of olive oil,' he answered. 'Here is your account,' the manager told him; 'sit down and write fifty.' [7]Then he asked another one, 'And you–how much do you owe?' 'A thousand bushels of wheat,' he answered. 'Here is your account,' the manager told him; 'write eight hundred.' [8]As a result the master of this dishonest manager praised him for doing such a shrewd thing; because the people of this world are much more shrewd in handling their affairs than the people who belong to the light."

[9]And Jesus went on to say, "And so I tell you: make friends for yourselves with worldly wealth, so that when it gives out, you will be welcomed in the

eternal home. [10]Whoever is faithful in small matters will be faithful in large ones; whoever is dishonest in small matters will be dishonest in large ones. [11]If, then, you have not been faithful in handling worldly wealth, how can you be trusted with true wealth? [12]And if you have not been faithful with what belongs to someone else, who will give you what belongs to you?

[13]"No servant can be the slave of two masters; such a slave will hate one and love the other or will be loyal to one and despise the other. You cannot serve both God and money."

## SOME SAYINGS OF JESUS

[14]When the Pharisees heard all this, they made fun of Jesus, because they loved money. [15]Jesus said to them, "You are the ones who make yourselves look right in other people's sight, but God knows your hearts. For the things that are considered of great value by people are worth nothing in God's sight.

[16]"The Law of Moses and the writings of the prophets were in effect up to the time of John the Baptist; since then the Good News about the Kingdom of God is being told, and everyone forces their way in. [17]But it is easier for heaven and earth to disappear than for the smallest detail of the Law to be done away with.

[18]"Any man who divorces his wife and marries another woman commits adultery; and the man who marries a divorced woman commits adultery.

## THE RICH MAN AND LAZARUS

[19]"There was once a rich man who dressed in the most expensive clothes and lived in great luxury every day. [20]There was also a poor man named Lazarus, covered with sores, who used to be brought to the rich man's door, [21]hoping to eat the bits of food that fell from the rich man's table. Even the dogs would come and lick his sores. [22]The poor man died and was carried by the angels to sit beside Abraham at the feast in heaven. The rich man died and was buried, [23]and in Hades, where he was in great pain, he looked up and saw Abraham, far away, with Lazarus at his side. [24]So he called out, 'Father Abraham! Take pity on me, and send Lazarus to dip his finger in some water and cool off my tongue, because I am in great pain in this fire!' [25]But Abraham said, 'Remember, my son, that in your lifetime you were given all the good things, while Lazarus got all the bad things. But now he is enjoying himself here, while you are in pain. [26]Besides all that, there is a deep pit lying between us, so that those who want to cross over from here to you cannot do so, nor can anyone cross over to us from where you are.' [27]The rich man said, 'Then I beg you, father Abraham, send Lazarus to my father's house, [28]where I have five brothers. Let him go and warn them so that they, at least, will not come to this place of pain.' [29]Abraham said, 'Your brothers have Moses and the prophets to warn them; your brothers should listen to what they say.' [30]The rich man answered, 'That is not enough, father Abraham! But if someone were to rise from death and go to them, then they would turn from their sins.' [31]But Abraham said, 'If they will not listen to Moses and the prophets, they will not be convinced even if someone were to rise from death.' "

## SIN

**17** Jesus said to his disciples, "Things that make people fall into sin are bound to happen, but how terrible for the one who makes them happen! [2]It would be better for him if a large millstone were tied around his neck and he were thrown into the sea than for him to cause one of these little ones to sin. <sup>3</sup>So watch what you do!

"If your brother sins, rebuke him, and if he repents, forgive him. <sup>4</sup>If he sins against you seven times in one day, and each time he comes to you saying, 'I repent,' you must forgive him."

## FAITH

<sup>5</sup>The apostles said to the Lord, "Make our faith greater."

<sup>6</sup>The Lord answered, "If you had faith as big as a mustard seed, you could say to this mulberry tree, 'Pull yourself up by the roots and plant yourself in the sea!' and it would obey you.

## A SERVANT'S DUTY

<sup>7</sup>"Suppose one of you has a servant who is plowing or looking after the sheep. When he comes in from the field, do you tell him to hurry along and eat his meal? <sup>8</sup>Of course not! Instead, you say to him, 'Get my supper ready, then put on your apron and wait on me while I eat and drink; after that you may have your meal.' <sup>9</sup>The servant does not deserve thanks for obeying orders, does he? <sup>10</sup>It is the same with you; when you have done all you have been told to do, say, 'We are ordinary servants; we have only done our duty.' "

## JESUS HEALS TEN MEN

<sup>11</sup>As Jesus made his way to Jerusalem, he went along the border between Samaria and Galilee. <sup>12</sup>He was going into a village when he was met by ten men suffering from a dreaded skin disease. They stood at a distance <sup>13</sup>and shouted, "Jesus! Master! Have pity on us!"

<sup>14</sup>Jesus saw them and said to them, "Go and let the priests examine you."

On the way they were made clean. <sup>15</sup>When one of them saw that he was healed, he came back, praising God in a loud voice. <sup>16</sup>He threw himself to the ground at Jesus' feet and thanked him. The man was a Samaritan. <sup>17</sup>Jesus spoke up, "There were ten who were healed; where are the other nine? <sup>18</sup>Why is this foreigner the only one who came back to give thanks to God?" <sup>19</sup>And Jesus said to him, "Get up and go; your faith has made you well."

## THE COMING OF THE KINGDOM

<sup>20</sup>Some Pharisees asked Jesus when the Kingdom of God would come. His answer was, "The Kingdom of God does not come in such a way as to be seen. <sup>21</sup>No one will say, 'Look, here it is!' or, 'There it is!'; because the Kingdom of God is within you."

<sup>22</sup>Then he said to the disciples, "The time will come when you will wish you could see one of the days of the Son of Man, but you will not see it. <sup>23</sup>There will be those who will say to you, 'Look, over there!' or, 'Look, over here!' But don't go out looking for it. <sup>24</sup>As the lightning flashes across the sky and lights it up from one side to the other, so will the Son of Man be in his day. <sup>25</sup>But first he must suffer much and be rejected by the people of this day. <sup>26</sup>As it was in the time of Noah so shall it be in the days of the Son of Man. <sup>27</sup>Everybody kept on eating and drinking, and men and women married, up to the very day Noah went into the boat and the flood came and killed them all. <sup>28</sup>It will be as it was in the time of Lot. Everybody kept on eating and drinking, buying and selling, planting and building. <sup>29</sup>On the day Lot left Sodom, fire and sulfur rained down from heaven and killed them all. <sup>30</sup>That is how it will be on the day the Son of Man is revealed.

<sup>31</sup>"On that day someone who is on the roof of a house must not go down into the house to get any belongings; in the same way anyone who is out in

the field must not go back to the house. [32]Remember Lot's wife! [33]Those who try to save their own life will lose it; those who lose their life will save it. [34]On that night, I tell you, there will be two people sleeping in the same bed: one will be taken away, the other will be left behind. [35]Two women will be grinding meal together: one will be taken away, the other will be left behind." [[36]]

[37]The disciples asked him, "Where, Lord?"

Jesus answered, "Wherever there is a dead body, the vultures will gather."

### THE PARABLE OF THE WIDOW AND THE JUDGE

18 Then Jesus told his disciples a parable to teach them that they should always pray and never become discouraged. [2]"In a certain town there was a judge who neither feared God nor respected people. [3]And there was a widow in that same town who kept coming to him and pleading for her rights, saying, 'Help me against my opponent!' [4]For a long time the judge refused to act, but at last he said to himself, 'Even though I don't fear God or respect people, [5]yet because of all the trouble this widow is giving me, I will see to it that she gets her rights. If I don't, she will keep on coming and finally wear me out!' "

[6]And the Lord continued, "Listen to what that corrupt judge said. [7]Now, will God not judge in favor of his own people who cry to him day and night for help? Will he be slow to help them? [8]I tell you, he will judge in their favor and do it quickly. But will the Son of Man find faith on earth when he comes?"

### THE PARABLE OF THE PHARISEE AND THE TAX COLLECTOR

[9]Jesus also told this parable to people who were sure of their own goodness and despised everybody else. [10]"Once there were two men who went up to the Temple to pray: one was a Pharisee, the other a tax collector. [11]The Pharisee stood apart by himself and prayed, 'I thank you, God, that I am not greedy, dishonest, or an adulterer, like everybody else. I thank you that I am not like that tax collector over there. [12]I fast two days a week, and I give you one tenth of all my income.' [13]But the tax collector stood at a distance and would not even raise his face to heaven, but beat on his breast and said, 'God, have pity on me, a sinner!' [14]I tell you," said Jesus, "the tax collector, and not the Pharisee, was in the right with God when he went home. For those who make themselves great will be humbled, and those who humble themselves will be made great."

### JESUS BLESSES LITTLE CHILDREN

[15]Some people brought their babies to Jesus for him to place his hands on them. The disciples saw them and scolded them for doing so, [16]but Jesus called the children to him and said, "Let the children come to me and do not stop them, because the Kingdom of God belongs to such as these. [17]Remember this! Whoever does not receive the Kingdom of God like a child will never enter it."

### THE RICH MAN

[18]A Jewish leader asked Jesus, "Good Teacher, what must I do to receive eternal life?"

[19]"Why do you call me good?" Jesus asked him. "No one is good except God alone. [20]You know the commandments: 'Do not commit adultery; do not commit murder; do not steal; do not accuse anyone falsely; respect your father and your mother.' "

[21]The man replied, "Ever since I was young, I have obeyed all these commandments."

<sup>22</sup>When Jesus heard this, he said to him, "There is still one more thing you need to do. Sell all you have and give the money to the poor, and you will have riches in heaven; then come and follow me." <sup>23</sup>But when the man heard this, he became very sad, because he was very rich.

<sup>24</sup>Jesus saw that he was sad and said, "How hard it is for rich people to enter the Kingdom of God! <sup>25</sup>It is much harder for a rich person to enter the Kingdom of God than for a camel to go through the eye of a needle."

<sup>26</sup>The people who heard him asked, "Who, then, can be saved?"

<sup>27</sup>Jesus answered, "What is humanly impossible is possible for God."

<sup>28</sup>Then Peter said, "Look! We have left our homes to follow you."

<sup>29</sup>"Yes," Jesus said to them, "and I assure you that anyone who leaves home or wife or brothers or parents or children for the sake of the Kingdom of God <sup>30</sup>will receive much more in this present age and eternal life in the age to come."

## JESUS SPEAKS A THIRD TIME ABOUT HIS DEATH

<sup>31</sup>Jesus took the twelve disciples aside and said to them, "Listen! We are going to Jerusalem where everything the prophets wrote about the Son of Man will come true. <sup>32</sup>He will be handed over to the Gentiles, who will make fun of him, insult him, and spit on him. <sup>33</sup>They will whip him and kill him, but three days later he will rise to life."

<sup>34</sup>But the disciples did not understand any of these things; the meaning of the words was hidden from them, and they did not know what Jesus was talking about.

## JESUS HEALS A BLIND BEGGAR

<sup>35</sup>As Jesus was coming near Jericho, there was a blind man sitting by the road, begging. <sup>36</sup>When he heard the crowd passing by, he asked, "What is this?"

<sup>37</sup>"Jesus of Nazareth is passing by," they told him.

<sup>38</sup>He cried out, "Jesus! Son of David! Have mercy on me!"

<sup>39</sup>The people in front scolded him and told him to be quiet. But he shouted even more loudly, "Son of David! Have mercy on me!"

<sup>40</sup>So Jesus stopped and ordered the blind man to be brought to him. When he came near, Jesus asked him, <sup>41</sup>"What do you want me to do for you?"

"Sir," he answered, "I want to see again."

<sup>42</sup>Jesus said to him, "Then see! Your faith has made you well."

<sup>43</sup>At once he was able to see, and he followed Jesus, giving thanks to God. When the crowd saw it, they all praised God.

## JESUS AND ZACCHAEUS

19 Jesus went on into Jericho and was passing through. <sup>2</sup>There was a chief tax collector there named Zacchaeus, who was rich. <sup>3</sup>He was trying to see who Jesus was, but he was a little man and could not see Jesus because of the crowd. <sup>4</sup>So he ran ahead of the crowd and climbed a sycamore tree to see Jesus, who was going to pass that way. <sup>5</sup>When Jesus came to that place, he looked up and said to Zacchaeus, "Hurry down, Zacchaeus, because I must stay in your house today."

<sup>6</sup>Zacchaeus hurried down and welcomed him with great joy. <sup>7</sup>All the people who saw it started grumbling, "This man has gone as a guest to the home of a sinner!"

<sup>8</sup>Zacchaeus stood up and said to the Lord, "Listen, sir! I will give half my belongings to the poor, and if I have

cheated anyone, I will pay back four times as much."

⁹Jesus said to him, "Salvation has come to this house today, for this man, also, is a descendant of Abraham. ¹⁰The Son of Man came to seek and to save the lost."

### THE PARABLE OF THE GOLD COINS

¹¹While the people were listening to this, Jesus continued and told them a parable. He was now almost at Jerusalem, and they supposed that the Kingdom of God was just about to appear. ¹²So he said, "There was once a man of high rank who was going to a country far away to be made king, after which he planned to come back home. ¹³Before he left, he called his ten servants and gave them each a gold coin and told them, 'See what you can earn with this while I am gone.' ¹⁴Now, his own people hated him, and so they sent messengers after him to say, 'We don't want this man to be our king.'

¹⁵"The man was made king and came back. At once he ordered his servants to appear before him, in order to find out how much they had earned. ¹⁶The first one came and said, 'Sir, I have earned ten gold coins with the one you gave me.' ¹⁷'Well done,' he said; 'you are a good servant! Since you were faithful in small matters, I will put you in charge of ten cities.' ¹⁸The second servant came and said, 'Sir, I have earned five gold coins with the one you gave me.' ¹⁹To this one he said, 'You will be in charge of five cities.' ²⁰Another servant came and said, 'Sir, here is your gold coin; I kept it hidden in a handkerchief. ²¹I was afraid of you, because you are a hard man. You take what is not yours and reap what you did not plant.' ²²He said to him, 'You bad servant! I will use your own words to condemn you! You know that I am a hard man, taking what is not mine and reaping

what I have not planted. ²³Well, then, why didn't you put my money in the bank? Then I would have received it back with interest when I returned.' ²⁴Then he said to those who were standing there, 'Take the gold coin away from him and give it to the servant who has ten coins.' ²⁵But they said to him, 'Sir, he already has ten coins!' ²⁶'I tell you,' he replied, 'that to those who have something, even more will be given; but those who have nothing, even the little that they have will be taken away from them. ²⁷Now, as for those enemies of mine who did not want me to be their king, bring them here and kill them in my presence!' "

### THE TRIUMPHANT APPROACH TO JERUSALEM

²⁸After Jesus said this, he went on in front of them toward Jerusalem. ²⁹As he came near Bethphage and Bethany at the Mount of Olives, he sent two disciples ahead ³⁰with these instructions: "Go to the village there ahead of you; as you go in, you will find a colt tied up that has never been ridden. Untie it and bring it here. ³¹If someone asks you why you are untying it, tell him that the Master needs it."

³²They went on their way and found everything just as Jesus had told them. ³³As they were untying the colt, its owners said to them, "Why are you untying it?"

³⁴"The Master needs it," they answered, ³⁵and they took the colt to Jesus. Then they threw their cloaks over the animal and helped Jesus get on. ³⁶As he rode on, people spread their cloaks on the road.

³⁷When he came near Jerusalem, at the place where the road went down the Mount of Olives, the large crowd of his disciples began to thank God and praise him in loud voices for all the great things that they had seen: ³⁸"God bless the king who comes in

the name of the Lord! Peace in heaven and glory to God!"

³⁹Then some of the Pharisees in the crowd spoke to Jesus. "Teacher," they said, "command your disciples to be quiet!"

⁴⁰Jesus answered, "I tell you that if they keep quiet, the stones themselves will start shouting."

### JESUS WEEPS OVER JERUSALEM

⁴¹He came closer to the city, and when he saw it, he wept over it, ⁴²saying, "If you only knew today what is needed for peace! But now you cannot see it! ⁴³The time will come when your enemies will surround you with barricades, blockade you, and close in on you from every side. ⁴⁴They will completely destroy you and the people within your walls; not a single stone will they leave in its place, because you did not recognize the time when God came to save you!"

### JESUS GOES TO THE TEMPLE

⁴⁵Then Jesus went into the Temple and began to drive out the merchants, ⁴⁶saying to them, "It is written in the Scriptures that God said, 'My Temple will be a house of prayer.' But you have turned it into a hideout for thieves!"

⁴⁷Every day Jesus taught in the Temple. The chief priests, the teachers of the Law, and the leaders of the people wanted to kill him, ⁴⁸but they could not find a way to do it, because all the people kept listening to him, not wanting to miss a single word.

### THE QUESTION ABOUT JESUS' AUTHORITY

20 One day when Jesus was in the Temple teaching the people and preaching the Good News, the chief priests and the teachers of the Law, together with the elders, came ²and said to him, "Tell us, what right

do you have to do these things? Who gave you such right?"

³Jesus answered them, "Now let me ask you a question. Tell me, ⁴did John's right to baptize come from God or from human beings?"

⁵They started to argue among themselves, "What shall we say? If we say, 'From God,' he will say, 'Why, then, did you not believe John?' ⁶But if we say, 'From human beings,' this whole crowd here will stone us, because they are convinced that John was a prophet." ⁷So they answered, "We don't know where it came from."

⁸And Jesus said to them, "Neither will I tell you, then, by what right I do these things."

### THE PARABLE OF THE TENANTS IN THE VINEYARD

⁹Then Jesus told the people this parable: "There was once a man who planted a vineyard, rented it out to tenants, and then left home for a long time. ¹⁰When the time came to gather the grapes, he sent a slave to the tenants to receive from them his share of the harvest. But the tenants beat the slave and sent him back without a thing. ¹¹So he sent another slave; but the tenants beat him also, treated him shamefully, and sent him back without a thing. ¹²Then he sent a third slave; the tenants wounded him, too, and threw him out. ¹³Then the owner of the vineyard said, 'What shall I do? I will send my own dear son; surely they will respect him!' ¹⁴But when the tenants saw him, they said to one another, 'This is the owner's son. Let's kill him, and his property will be ours!' ¹⁵So they threw him out of the vineyard and killed him.

"What, then, will the owner of the vineyard do to the tenants?" Jesus asked. ¹⁶"He will come and kill those men, and turn the vineyard over to other tenants."

When the people heard this, they said, "Surely not!"

[17]Jesus looked at them and asked, "What, then, does this scripture mean?

'The stone which the builders
rejected as worthless
turned out to be
the most important of all.'

[18]Everyone who falls on that stone will be cut to pieces; and if that stone falls on someone, that person will be crushed to dust."

## THE QUESTION ABOUT PAYING TAXES

[19]The teachers of the Law and the chief priests tried to arrest Jesus on the spot, because they knew that he had told this parable against them; but they were afraid of the people. [20]So they looked for an opportunity. They bribed some men to pretend they were sincere, and they sent them to trap Jesus with questions, so that they could hand him over to the authority and power of the Roman Governor. [21]These spies said to Jesus, "Teacher, we know that what you say and teach is right. We know that you pay no attention to anyone's status, but teach the truth about God's will for people. [22]Tell us, is it against our Law for us to pay taxes to the Roman Emperor, or not?"

[23]But Jesus saw through their trick and said to them, [24]"Show me a silver coin. Whose face and name are these on it?"

"The Emperor's," they answered.

[25]So Jesus said, "Well, then, pay to the Emperor what belongs to the Emperor, and pay to God what belongs to God."

[26]There before the people they could not catch him in a thing, so they kept quiet, amazed at his answer.

## THE QUESTION ABOUT RISING FROM DEATH

[27]Then some Sadducees, who say that people will not rise from death, came to Jesus and said, [28]"Teacher, Moses wrote this law for us: 'If a man dies and leaves a wife but no children, that man's brother must marry the widow so that they can have children who will be considered the dead man's children.' [29]Once there were seven brothers; the oldest got married and died without having children. [30]Then the second one married the woman, [31]and then the third. The same thing happened to all seven–they died without having children. [32]Last of all, the woman died. [33]Now, on the day when the dead rise to life, whose wife will she be? All seven of them had married her."

[34]Jesus answered them, "The men and women of this age marry, [35]but the men and women who are worthy to rise from death and live in the age to come will not then marry. [36]They will be like angels and cannot die. They are the children of God, because they have risen from death. [37]And Moses clearly proves that the dead are raised to life. In the passage about the burning bush he speaks of the Lord as 'the God of Abraham, the God of Isaac, and the God of Jacob.' [38]He is the God of the living, not of the dead, for to him all are alive."

[39]Some of the teachers of the Law spoke up, "A good answer, Teacher!" [40]For they did not dare ask him any more questions.

## THE QUESTION ABOUT THE MESSIAH

[41]Jesus asked them, "How can it be said that the Messiah will be the descendant of David? [42]For David himself says in the book of Psalms,

'The Lord said to my Lord:
Sit here at my right side
[43]until I put your enemies
as a footstool under your feet.'

⁴⁴David called him 'Lord'; how, then, can the Messiah be David's descendant?"

## JESUS WARNS AGAINST THE TEACHERS OF THE LAW

⁴⁵As all the people listened to him, Jesus said to his disciples, ⁴⁶"Be on your guard against the teachers of the Law, who like to walk around in their long robes and love to be greeted with respect in the marketplace; who choose the reserved seats in the synagogues and the best places at feasts; ⁴⁷who take advantage of widows and rob them of their homes, and then make a show of saying long prayers! Their punishment will be all the worse!"

## THE WIDOW'S OFFERING

21 Jesus looked around and saw rich people dropping their gifts in the Temple treasury, ²and he also saw a very poor widow dropping in two little copper coins. ³He said, "I tell you that this poor widow put in more than all the others. ⁴For the others offered their gifts from what they had to spare of their riches; but she, poor as she is, gave all she had to live on."

## JESUS SPEAKS OF THE DESTRUCTION OF THE TEMPLE

⁵Some of the disciples were talking about the Temple, how beautiful it looked with its fine stones and the gifts offered to God. Jesus said, ⁶"All this you see–the time will come when not a single stone here will be left in its place; every one will be thrown down."

## TROUBLES AND PERSECUTIONS

⁷"Teacher," they asked, "when will this be? And what will happen in order to show that the time has come for it to take place?"

⁸Jesus said, "Watch out; don't be fooled. Many men, claiming to speak for me, will come and say, 'I am he!' and, 'The time has come!' But don't follow them. ⁹Don't be afraid when you hear of wars and revolutions; such things must happen first, but they do not mean that the end is near."

¹⁰He went on to say, "Countries will fight each other; kingdoms will attack one another. ¹¹There will be terrible earthquakes, famines, and plagues everywhere; there will be strange and terrifying things coming from the sky. ¹²Before all these things take place, however, you will be arrested and persecuted; you will be handed over to be tried in synagogues and be put in prison; you will be brought before kings and rulers for my sake. ¹³This will be your chance to tell the Good News. ¹⁴Make up your minds ahead of time not to worry about how you will defend yourselves, ¹⁵because I will give you such words and wisdom that none of your enemies will be able to refute or contradict what you say. ¹⁶You will be handed over by your parents, your brothers, your relatives, and your friends; and some of you will be put to death. ¹⁷Everyone will hate you because of me. ¹⁸But not a single hair from your heads will be lost. ¹⁹Stand firm, and you will save yourselves.

## JESUS SPEAKS OF THE DESTRUCTION OF JERUSALEM

²⁰"When you see Jerusalem surrounded by armies, then you will know that it will soon be destroyed. ²¹Then those who are in Judea must run away to the hills; those who are in the city must leave, and those who are out in the country must not go into the city. ²²For those will be 'The Days of Punishment,' to make come true all that the Scriptures say. ²³How terrible it will be in those days for women who are pregnant and for mothers

with little babies! Terrible distress will come upon this land, and God's punishment will fall on this people. [24]Some will be killed by the sword, and others will be taken as prisoners to all countries; and the heathen will trample over Jerusalem until their time is up.

### THE COMING OF THE SON OF MAN

[25]"There will be strange things happening to the sun, the moon, and the stars. On earth whole countries will be in despair, afraid of the roar of the sea and the raging tides. [26]People will faint from fear as they wait for what is coming over the whole earth, for the powers in space will be driven from their courses. [27]Then the Son of Man will appear, coming in a cloud with great power and glory. [28]When these things begin to happen, stand up and raise your heads, because your salvation is near."

### THE LESSON OF THE FIG TREE

[29]Then Jesus told them this parable: "Think of the fig tree and all the other trees. [30]When you see their leaves beginning to appear, you know that summer is near. [31]In the same way, when you see these things happening, you will know that the Kingdom of God is about to come.

[32]"Remember that all these things will take place before the people now living have all died. [33]Heaven and earth will pass away, but my words will never pass away.

### THE NEED TO WATCH

[34]"Be careful not to let yourselves become occupied with too much feasting and drinking and with the worries of this life, or that Day may suddenly catch you [35]like a trap. For it will come upon all people everywhere on earth. [36]Be on watch and pray always that you will have the strength to go safely through all those things

that will happen and to stand before the Son of Man."

[37]Jesus spent those days teaching in the Temple, and when evening came, he would go out and spend the night on the Mount of Olives. [38]Early each morning all the people went to the Temple to listen to him.

### THE PLOT AGAINST JESUS

22 The time was near for the Festival of Unleavened Bread, which is called the Passover. [2]The chief priests and the teachers of the Law were afraid of the people, and so they were trying to find a way of putting Jesus to death secretly.

### JUDAS AGREES TO BETRAY JESUS

[3]Then Satan entered into Judas, called Iscariot, who was one of the twelve disciples. [4]So Judas went off and spoke with the chief priests and the officers of the Temple guard about how he could betray Jesus to them. [5]They were pleased and offered to pay him money. [6]Judas agreed to it and started looking for a good chance to hand Jesus over to them without the people knowing about it.

### JESUS PREPARES TO EAT THE PASSOVER MEAL

[7]The day came during the Festival of Unleavened Bread when the lambs for the Passover meal were to be killed. [8]Jesus sent Peter and John with these instructions: "Go and get the Passover meal ready for us to eat."

[9]"Where do you want us to get it ready?" they asked him.

[10]He answered, "As you go into the city, a man carrying a jar of water will meet you. Follow him into the house that he enters, [11]and say to the owner of the house: 'The Teacher says to you, Where is the room where my disciples and I will eat the Passover meal?' [12]He will show you a large

furnished room upstairs, where you will get everything ready."

¹³They went off and found everything just as Jesus had told them, and they prepared the Passover meal.

## THE LORD'S SUPPER

¹⁴When the hour came, Jesus took his place at the table with the apostles. ¹⁵He said to them, "I have wanted so much to eat this Passover meal with you before I suffer! ¹⁶For I tell you, I will never eat it until it is given its full meaning in the Kingdom of God."

¹⁷Then Jesus took a cup, gave thanks to God, and said, "Take this and share it among yourselves. ¹⁸I tell you that from now on I will not drink this wine until the Kingdom of God comes."

¹⁹Then he took a piece of bread, gave thanks to God, broke it, and gave it to them, saying, "This is my body, which is given for you. Do this in memory of me." ²⁰In the same way, he gave them the cup after the supper, saying, "This cup is God's new covenant sealed with my blood, which is poured out for you.

²¹"But, look! The one who betrays me is here at the table with me! ²²The Son of Man will die as God has decided, but how terrible for that man who betrays him!"

²³Then they began to ask among themselves which one of them it could be who was going to do this.

## THE ARGUMENT ABOUT GREATNESS

²⁴An argument broke out among the disciples as to which one of them should be thought of as the greatest. ²⁵Jesus said to them, "The kings of the pagans have power over their people, and the rulers claim the title 'Friends of the People.' ²⁶But this is not the way it is with you; rather, the greatest one among you must be like the youngest, and the leader must be like the servant. ²⁷Who is greater, the one who sits down to eat or the one who serves? The one who sits down, of course. But I am among you as one who serves.

²⁸"You have stayed with me all through my trials; ²⁹and just as my Father has given me the right to rule, so I will give you the same right. ³⁰You will eat and drink at my table in my Kingdom, and you will sit on thrones to rule over the twelve tribes of Israel.

## JESUS PREDICTS PETER'S DENIAL

³¹"Simon, Simon! Listen! Satan has received permission to test all of you, to separate the good from the bad, as a farmer separates the wheat from the chaff. ³²But I have prayed for you, Simon, that your faith will not fail. And when you turn back to me, you must strengthen your brothers."

³³Peter answered, "Lord, I am ready to go to prison with you and to die with you!"

³⁴"I tell you, Peter," Jesus said, "the rooster will not crow tonight until you have said three times that you do not know me."

## PURSE, BAG, AND SWORD

³⁵Then Jesus asked his disciples, "When I sent you out that time without purse, bag, or shoes, did you lack anything?"

"Not a thing," they answered.

³⁶"But now," Jesus said, "whoever has a purse or a bag must take it; and whoever does not have a sword must sell his coat and buy one. ³⁷For I tell you that the scripture which says, 'He shared the fate of criminals,' must come true about me, because what was written about me is coming true."

³⁸The disciples said, "Look! Here are two swords, Lord!"

"That is enough!" he replied.

## JESUS PRAYS
### ON THE MOUNT OF OLIVES

<sup>39</sup>Jesus left the city and went, as he usually did, to the Mount of Olives; and the disciples went with him. <sup>40</sup>When he arrived at the place, he said to them, "Pray that you will not fall into temptation."

<sup>41</sup>Then he went off from them about the distance of a stone's throw and knelt down and prayed. <sup>42</sup>"Father," he said, "if you will, take this cup of suffering away from me. Not my will, however, but your will be done." <sup>43</sup>An angel from heaven appeared to him and strengthened him. <sup>44</sup>In great anguish he prayed even more fervently; his sweat was like drops of blood falling to the ground.

<sup>45</sup>Rising from his prayer, he went back to the disciples and found them asleep, worn out by their grief. <sup>46</sup>He said to them, "Why are you sleeping? Get up and pray that you will not fall into temptation."

### THE ARREST OF JESUS

<sup>47</sup>Jesus was still speaking when a crowd arrived, led by Judas, one of the twelve disciples. He came up to Jesus to kiss him. <sup>48</sup>But Jesus said, "Judas, is it with a kiss that you betray the Son of Man?"

<sup>49</sup>When the disciples who were with Jesus saw what was going to happen, they asked, "Shall we use our swords, Lord?" <sup>50</sup>And one of them struck the High Priest's slave and cut off his right ear.

<sup>51</sup>But Jesus said, "Enough of this!" He touched the man's ear and healed him.

<sup>52</sup>Then Jesus said to the chief priests and the officers of the Temple guard and the elders who had come there to get him, "Did you have to come with swords and clubs, as though I were an outlaw? <sup>53</sup>I was with you in the Temple every day, and you did not try to arrest me. But this is your hour to act, when the power of darkness rules."

### PETER DENIES JESUS

<sup>54</sup>They arrested Jesus and took him away into the house of the High Priest; and Peter followed at a distance. <sup>55</sup>A fire had been lit in the center of the courtyard, and Peter joined those who were sitting around it. <sup>56</sup>When one of the servant women saw him sitting there at the fire, she looked straight at him and said, "This man too was with Jesus!"

<sup>57</sup>But Peter denied it, "Woman, I don't even know him!"

<sup>58</sup>After a little while a man noticed Peter and said, "You are one of them, too!"

But Peter answered, "Man, I am not!"

<sup>59</sup>And about an hour later another man insisted strongly, "There isn't any doubt that this man was with Jesus, because he also is a Galilean!"

<sup>60</sup>But Peter answered, "Man, I don't know what you are talking about!"

At once, while he was still speaking, a rooster crowed. <sup>61</sup>The Lord turned around and looked straight at Peter, and Peter remembered that the Lord had said to him, "Before the rooster crows tonight, you will say three times that you do not know me." <sup>62</sup>Peter went out and wept bitterly.

### JESUS IS MOCKED AND BEATEN

<sup>63</sup>The men who were guarding Jesus made fun of him and beat him. <sup>64</sup>They blindfolded him and asked him, "Who hit you? Guess!" <sup>65</sup>And they said many other insulting things to him.

### JESUS BEFORE THE COUNCIL

<sup>66</sup>When day came, the elders, the chief priests, and the teachers of the

Law met together, and Jesus was brought before the Council. [67]"Tell us," they said, "are you the Messiah?"

He answered, "If I tell you, you will not believe me; [68]and if I ask you a question, you will not answer. [69]But from now on the Son of Man will be seated at the right side of Almighty God."

[70]They all said, "Are you, then, the Son of God?"

He answered them, "You say that I am."

[71]And they said, "We don't need any witnesses! We ourselves have heard what he said!"

### JESUS BEFORE PILATE

23 The whole group rose up and took Jesus before Pilate, [2]where they began to accuse him: "We caught this man misleading our people, telling them not to pay taxes to the Emperor and claiming that he himself is the Messiah, a king."

[3]Pilate asked him, "Are you the king of the Jews?"

"So you say," answered Jesus.

[4]Then Pilate said to the chief priests and the crowds, "I find no reason to condemn this man."

[5]But they insisted even more strongly, "With his teaching he is starting a riot among the people all through Judea. He began in Galilee and now has come here."

### JESUS BEFORE HEROD

[6]When Pilate heard this, he asked, "Is this man a Galilean?" [7]When he learned that Jesus was from the region ruled by Herod, he sent him to Herod, who was also in Jerusalem at that time. [8]Herod was very pleased when he saw Jesus, because he had heard about him and had been wanting to see him for a long time. He was hoping to see Jesus perform some

miracle. [9]So Herod asked Jesus many questions, but Jesus made no answer. [10]The chief priests and the teachers of the Law stepped forward and made strong accusations against Jesus. [11]Herod and his soldiers made fun of Jesus and treated him with contempt; then they put a fine robe on him and sent him back to Pilate. [12]On that very day Herod and Pilate became friends; before this they had been enemies.

### JESUS IS SENTENCED TO DEATH

[13]Pilate called together the chief priests, the leaders, and the people, [14]and said to them, "You brought this man to me and said that he was misleading the people. Now, I have examined him here in your presence, and I have not found him guilty of any of the crimes you accuse him of. [15]Nor did Herod find him guilty, for he sent him back to us. There is nothing this man has done to deserve death. [16]So I will have him whipped and let him go."

[18]The whole crowd cried out, "Kill him! Set Barabbas free for us!" ([19]Barabbas had been put in prison for a riot that had taken place in the city, and for murder.)

[20]Pilate wanted to set Jesus free, so he appealed to the crowd again. [21]But they shouted back, "Crucify him! Crucify him!"

[22]Pilate said to them the third time, "But what crime has he committed? I cannot find anything he has done to deserve death! I will have him whipped and set him free."

[23]But they kept on shouting at the top of their voices that Jesus should be crucified, and finally their shouting succeeded. [24]So Pilate passed the sentence on Jesus that they were asking for. [25]He set free the man they wanted, the one who had been put in prison for riot and murder, and he handed Jesus over for them to do as they wished.

## JESUS IS CRUCIFIED

<sup>26</sup>The soldiers led Jesus away, and as they were going, they met a man from Cyrene named Simon who was coming into the city from the country. They seized him, put the cross on him, and made him carry it behind Jesus.

<sup>27</sup>A large crowd of people followed him; among them were some women who were weeping and wailing for him. <sup>28</sup>Jesus turned to them and said, "Women of Jerusalem! Don't cry for me, but for yourselves and your children. <sup>29</sup>For the days are coming when people will say, 'How lucky are the women who never had children, who never bore babies, who never nursed them!' <sup>30</sup>That will be the time when people will say to the mountains, 'Fall on us!' and to the hills, 'Hide us!' <sup>31</sup>For if such things as these are done when the wood is green, what will happen when it is dry?"

<sup>32</sup>Two other men, both of them criminals, were also led out to be put to death with Jesus. <sup>33</sup>When they came to the place called "The Skull," they crucified Jesus there, and the two criminals, one on his right and the other on his left. <sup>34</sup>Jesus said, "Forgive them, Father! They don't know what they are doing."

They divided his clothes among themselves by throwing dice. <sup>35</sup>The people stood there watching while the Jewish leaders made fun of him: "He saved others; let him save himself if he is the Messiah whom God has chosen!"

<sup>36</sup>The soldiers also made fun of him: they came up to him and offered him cheap wine, <sup>37</sup>and said, "Save yourself if you are the king of the Jews!"

<sup>38</sup>Above him were written these words: "This is the King of the Jews."

<sup>39</sup>One of the criminals hanging there hurled insults at him: "Aren't you the Messiah? Save yourself and us!"

<sup>40</sup>The other one, however, rebuked him, saying, "Don't you fear God? You received the same sentence he did. <sup>41</sup>Ours, however, is only right, because we are getting what we deserve for what we did; but he has done no wrong." <sup>42</sup>And he said to Jesus, "Remember me, Jesus, when you come as King!"

<sup>43</sup>Jesus said to him, "I promise you that today you will be in Paradise with me."

## THE DEATH OF JESUS

<sup>44-45</sup>It was about twelve o'clock when the sun stopped shining and darkness covered the whole country until three o'clock; and the curtain hanging in the Temple was torn in two. <sup>46</sup>Jesus cried out in a loud voice, "Father! In your hands I place my spirit!" He said this and died.

<sup>47</sup>The army officer saw what had happened, and he praised God, saying, "Certainly he was a good man!"

<sup>48</sup>When the people who had gathered there to watch the spectacle saw what happened, they all went back home, beating their breasts in sorrow. <sup>49</sup>All those who knew Jesus personally, including the women who had followed him from Galilee, stood at a distance to watch.

## THE BURIAL OF JESUS

<sup>50-51</sup>There was a man named Joseph from Arimathea, a town in Judea. He was a good and honorable man, who was waiting for the coming of the Kingdom of God. Although he was a member of the Council, he had not agreed with their decision and action. <sup>52</sup>He went into the presence of Pilate and asked for the body of Jesus. <sup>53</sup>Then he took the body down, wrapped it in a linen sheet, and placed it in a tomb which had been dug out of

solid rock and which had never been used. ⁵⁴It was Friday, and the Sabbath was about to begin.

⁵⁵The women who had followed Jesus from Galilee went with Joseph and saw the tomb and how Jesus' body was placed in it. ⁵⁶Then they went back home and prepared the spices and perfumes for the body.

On the Sabbath they rested, as the Law commanded.

### THE RESURRECTION

24 Very early on Sunday morning the women went to the tomb, carrying the spices they had prepared. ²They found the stone rolled away from the entrance to the tomb, ³so they went in; but they did not find the body of the Lord Jesus. ⁴They stood there puzzled about this, when suddenly two men in bright shining clothes stood by them. ⁵Full of fear, the women bowed down to the ground, as the men said to them, "Why are you looking among the dead for one who is alive? ⁶He is not here; he has been raised. Remember what he said to you while he was in Galilee: ⁷'The Son of Man must be handed over to sinners, be crucified, and three days later rise to life.' "

⁸Then the women remembered his words, ⁹returned from the tomb, and told all these things to the eleven disciples and all the rest. ¹⁰The women were Mary Magdalene, Joanna, and Mary the mother of James; they and the other women with them told these things to the apostles. ¹¹But the apostles thought that what the women said was nonsense, and they did not believe them. ¹²But Peter got up and ran to the tomb; he bent down and saw the grave cloths but nothing else. Then he went back home amazed at what had happened.

### THE WALK TO EMMAUS

¹³On that same day two of Jesus' followers were going to a village named Emmaus, about seven miles from Jerusalem, ¹⁴and they were talking to each other about all the things that had happened. ¹⁵As they talked and discussed, Jesus himself drew near and walked along with them; ¹⁶they saw him, but somehow did not recognize him. ¹⁷Jesus said to them, "What are you talking about to each other, as you walk along?"

They stood still, with sad faces. ¹⁸One of them, named Cleopas, asked him, "Are you the only visitor in Jerusalem who doesn't know the things that have been happening there these last few days?"

¹⁹"What things?" he asked.

"The things that happened to Jesus of Nazareth," they answered. "This man was a prophet and was considered by God and by all the people to be powerful in everything he said and did. ²⁰Our chief priests and rulers handed him over to be sentenced to death, and he was crucified. ²¹And we had hoped that he would be the one who was going to set Israel free! Besides all that, this is now the third day since it happened. ²²Some of the women of our group surprised us; they went at dawn to the tomb, ²³but could not find his body. They came back saying they had seen a vision of angels who told them that he is alive. ²⁴Some of our group went to the tomb and found it exactly as the women had said, but they did not see him."

²⁵Then Jesus said to them, "How foolish you are, how slow you are to believe everything the prophets said! ²⁶Was it not necessary for the Messiah to suffer these things and then to enter his glory?" ²⁷And Jesus explained to them what was said about himself in all the Scriptures, beginning with the books of Moses and the writings of all the prophets.

²⁸As they came near the village to which they were going, Jesus acted as if he were going farther; ²⁹but they held him back, saying, "Stay with us; the day is almost over and it is getting dark." So he went in to stay with them. ³⁰He sat down to eat with them, took the bread, and said the blessing; then he broke the bread and gave it to them. ³¹Then their eyes were opened and they recognized him, but he disappeared from their sight. ³²They said to each other, "Wasn't it like a fire burning in us when he talked to us on the road and explained the Scriptures to us?"

³³They got up at once and went back to Jerusalem, where they found the eleven disciples gathered together with the others ³⁴and saying, "The Lord is risen indeed! He has appeared to Simon!"

³⁵The two then explained to them what had happened on the road, and how they had recognized the Lord when he broke the bread.

### JESUS APPEARS TO HIS DISCIPLES

³⁶While the two were telling them this, suddenly the Lord himself stood among them and said to them, "Peace be with you."

³⁷They were terrified, thinking that they were seeing a ghost. ³⁸But he said to them, "Why are you alarmed? Why are these doubts coming up in your minds? ³⁹Look at my hands and my feet, and see that it is I myself. Feel me, and you will know, for a ghost doesn't have flesh and bones, as you can see I have."

⁴⁰He said this and showed them his hands and his feet. ⁴¹They still could not believe, they were so full of joy and wonder; so he asked them, "Do you have anything here to eat?" ⁴²They gave him a piece of cooked fish, ⁴³which he took and ate in their presence.

⁴⁴Then he said to them, "These are the very things I told you about while I was still with you: everything written about me in the Law of Moses, the writings of the prophets, and the Psalms had to come true."

⁴⁵ Then he opened their minds to understand the Scriptures, ⁴⁶and said to them, "This is what is written: the Messiah must suffer and must rise from death three days later, ⁴⁷and in his name the message about repentance and the forgiveness of sins must be preached to all nations, beginning in Jerusalem. ⁴⁸You are witnesses of these things. ⁴⁹And I myself will send upon you what my Father has promised. But you must wait in the city until the power from above comes down upon you."

### JESUS IS TAKEN UP TO HEAVEN

⁵⁰Then he led them out of the city as far as Bethany, where he raised his hands and blessed them. ⁵¹As he was blessing them, he departed from them and was taken up into heaven. ⁵²They worshiped him and went back into Jerusalem, filled with great joy, ⁵³and spent all their time in the Temple giving thanks to God.

## IF YOU ARE LOOKING FOR...

# PSALMS
# AND
# PRAYERS

"Mary, Queen of peace, pray for us."
Painting by Bradi Barth.

## TRUE HAPPINESS

¹Happy are those
who reject the advice of evil people,
who do not follow the example of sinners
or join those who have no use for God.
²Instead, they find joy in obeying the Law of the Lord,
and they study it day and night.
³They are like trees that grow beside a stream,
that bear fruit at the right time,
and whose leaves do not dry up.
They succeed in everything they do.

⁴But evil people are not like this at all;
they are like straw that the wind blows away.
⁵Sinners will be condemned by God
and kept apart from God's own people.
⁶The righteous are guided and protected by the Lord,
but the evil are on the way to their doom.

## A PRAYER FOR HELP

¹How much longer will you forget me, Lord?
Forever?
How much longer will you hide
yourself from me?
²How long must I endure trouble?
How long will sorrow fill my heart day and night?
How long will my enemies triumph over me?

³Look at me, O Lord my God, and answer me.
Restore my strength; don't let me die.

⁴Don't let my enemies say, "We have defeated him."
Don't let them gloat over my downfall.

⁵I rely on your constant love;
I will be glad, because you will rescue me.
⁶I will sing to you, O Lord,
because you have been good to me.

## DAVID'S SONG OF VICTORY

¹How I love you, Lord!
You are my defender.
²The Lord is my protector;
he is my strong fortress.
My God is my protection,

and with him I am safe.
He protects me like a shield;
he defends me and keeps me safe.
[3]I call to the Lord,
and he saves me from my enemies.
Praise the Lord!

[4]The danger of death was all around me;
the waves of destruction rolled over me.
[5]The danger of death was around me,
and the grave set its trap for me.
[6]In my trouble I called to the Lord;
I called to my God for help.
In his temple he heard my voice;
he listened to my cry for help.

[16]The Lord reached down from above and took hold of me;
he pulled me out of the deep waters.
[17]He rescued me from my powerful enemies
and from all those who hate me–
they were too strong for me.

[18]When I was in trouble, they attacked me,
but the Lord protected me.
[19]He helped me out of danger;
he saved me because he was pleased with me.

[20]The Lord rewards me because I do what is right;
he blesses me because I am innocent.

[46]The Lord lives! Praise my defender!
Proclaim the greatness of the God who saves me.
[47]He gives me victory over my enemies;
he subdues the nations under me
[48]and saves me from my foes.

O Lord, you give me victory over my enemies
and protect me from violent people.
[49]And so I praise you among the nations;
I sing praises to you.

[50]God gives great victories to his king;
he shows constant love to the one he has chosen,
to David and his descendants forever.


## A CRY OF ANGUISH AND A SONG OF PRAISE

*PSALM 21 (22)*

[1]My God, my God, why have you abandoned me?
I have cried desperately for help,
but still it does not come.
[2]During the day I call to you, my God,
but you do not answer;
I call at night,

but get no rest.
³But you are enthroned as the Holy One,
the one whom Israel praises.
⁴Our ancestors put their trust in you;
they trusted you, and you saved them.
⁵They called to you and escaped from danger;
they trusted you and were not disappointed.

⁶But I am no longer a human being; I am a worm,
despised and scorned by everyone!
⁷All who see me make fun of me;
they stick out their tongues and shake their heads.
⁸"You relied on the Lord," they say.
"Why doesn't he save you?
If the Lord likes you,
why doesn't he help you?"

⁹It was you who brought me safely through birth,
and when I was a baby, you kept me safe.
¹⁰I have relied on you since the day I was born,
and you have always been my God.
¹¹Do not stay away from me!
Trouble is near,
and there is no one to help.

¹²Many enemies surround me like bulls;
they are all around me,
like fierce bulls from the land of Bashan.
¹³They open their mouths like lions,
roaring and tearing at me.

¹⁴My strength is gone,
gone like water spilled on the ground.
All my bones are out of joint;
my heart is like melted wax.
¹⁵My throat is as dry as dust,
and my tongue sticks to the roof of my mouth.
You have left me for dead in the dust.

¹⁶An evil gang is around me;
like a pack of dogs they close in on me;
they tear at my hands and feet.
¹⁷All my bones can be seen.
My enemies look at me and stare.
¹⁸They gamble for my clothes
and divide them among themselves.

¹⁹O Lord, don't stay away from me!
Come quickly to my rescue!
²⁰Save me from the sword;
save my life from these dogs.
²¹Rescue me from these lions;
I am helpless before these wild bulls.

²²I will tell my people what you have done;
I will praise you in their assembly:
²³"Praise him, you servants of the Lord!
Honor him, you descendants of Jacob!
Worship him, you people of Israel!
²⁴He does not neglect the poor or ignore their suffering;
he does not turn away from them,
but answers when they call for help."

²⁵In the full assembly I will praise you for what you have done;
in the presence of those who worship you
I will offer the sacrifices I promised.
²⁶The poor will eat as much as they want;
those who come to the Lord will praise him.
May they prosper forever!

²⁷All nations will remember the Lord.
From every part of the world they will turn to him;
all races will worship him.
²⁸The Lord is king,
and he rules the nations.

²⁹All proud people will bow down to him;
all mortals will bow down before him.
³⁰Future generations will serve him;
they will speak of the Lord to the coming generation.
³¹People not yet born will be told:
"The Lord saved his people."

## THE LORD OUR SHEPHERD

*PSALM 22 (23)*

¹The Lord is my shepherd;
I have everything I need.
²He lets me rest in fields of green grass
and leads me to quiet pools of fresh water.
³He gives me new strength.
He guides me in the right paths,
as he has promised.
⁴Even if I go through the deepest darkness,
I will not be afraid, Lord,
for you are with me.
Your shepherd's rod and staff protect me.

⁵You prepare a banquet for me,
where all my enemies can see me;
you welcome me as an honored guest
and fill my cup to the brim.
⁶I know that your goodness and love will be with me all my life;
and your house will be my home as long as I live.

## A PRAYER OF PRAISE

PSALM 26 (27)

[1]The Lord is my light and my salvation;
I will fear no one.
The Lord protects me from all danger;
I will never be afraid.

[2]When evil people attack me
and try to kill me,
they stumble and fall.
[3]Even if a whole army surrounds me,
I will not be afraid;
even if enemies attack me,
I will still trust God.

[4]I have asked the Lord for one thing;
one thing only do I want:
to live in the Lord's house all my life,
to marvel there at his goodness,
and to ask for his guidance.
[5]In times of trouble he will shelter me;
he will keep me safe in his Temple
and make me secure on a high rock.
[6]So I will triumph over my enemies around me.
With shouts of joy I will offer sacrifices in his Temple;
I will sing, I will praise the Lord.

[7]Hear me, Lord, when I call to you!
Be merciful and answer me!
[8]When you said, "Come worship me,"
I answered, "I will come, Lord."
[9]Don't hide yourself from me!

Don't be angry with me;
don't turn your servant away.
You have been my help;
don't leave me, don't abandon me,
O God, my savior.
[10]My father and mother may abandon me,
but the Lord will take care of me.

[11]Teach me, Lord, what you want me to do,
and lead me along a safe path,
because I have many enemies.
[12]Don't abandon me to my enemies,
who attack me with lies and threats.

[13]I know that I will live to see
the Lord's goodness in this present life.
[14]Trust in the Lord.
Have faith, do not despair.
Trust in the Lord.

## A Prayer of Thanksgiving

¹I praise you, Lord, because you have saved me
and kept my enemies from gloating over me.
²I cried to you for help, O Lord my God,
and you healed me;
³you kept me from the grave.
I was on my way to the depths below,
but you restored my life.

⁴Sing praise to the Lord,
all his faithful people!
Remember what the Holy One has done,
and give him thanks!
⁵His anger lasts only a moment,
his goodness for a lifetime.
Tears may flow in the night,
but joy comes in the morning.

⁶I felt secure and said to myself,
"I will never be defeated."
⁷You were good to me, Lord;
you protected me like a mountain fortress.
But then you hid yourself from me,
and I was afraid.

⁸I called to you, Lord;
I begged for your help:
⁹"What will you gain from my death?
What profit from my going to the grave?
Are dead people able to praise you?
Can they proclaim your unfailing goodness?
¹⁰Hear me, Lord, and be merciful!
Help me, Lord!"

¹¹You have changed my sadness into a joyful dance;
you have taken away my sorrow
and surrounded me with joy.
¹²So I will not be silent;
I will sing praise to you.
Lord, you are my God;
I will give you thanks forever.

## A Song of Praise

¹I waited patiently for the Lord's help;
then he listened to me and heard my cry.
²He pulled me out of a dangerous pit,
out of the deadly quicksand.
He set me safely on a rock
and made me secure.

³He taught me to sing a new song,
a song of praise to our God.
Many who see this will take warning
and will put their trust in the Lord.

⁴Happy are those who trust the Lord,
who do not turn to idols
or join those who worship false gods.
⁵You have done many things for us, O Lord our God;
there is no one like you!
You have made many wonderful plans for us.
I could never speak of them all–
their number is so great!

⁶You do not want sacrifices and offerings;
you do not ask for animals burned whole on the altar
or for sacrifices to take away sins.
Instead, you have given me ears to hear you,
⁷and so I answered, "Here I am;
your instructions for me are in the book of the Law.
⁸How I love to do your will, my God!
I keep your teaching in my heart."

⁹In the assembly of all your people, Lord,
I told the good news that you save us.
You know that I will never stop telling it.
¹⁰I have not kept the news of salvation to myself;
I have always spoken of your faithfulness and help.
In the assembly of all your people I have not been silent
about your loyalty and constant love.

¹¹Lord, I know you will never stop being merciful to me.
Your love and loyalty will always keep me safe.

¹²I am surrounded by many troubles–
too many to count!
My sins have caught up with me,
and I can no longer see;
they are more than the hairs of my head,
and I have lost my courage.
¹³Save me, Lord! Help me now!
¹⁴May those who try to kill me
be completely defeated and confused.

May those who are happy because of my troubles
be turned back and disgraced.
¹⁵May those who make fun of me
be dismayed by their defeat.

¹⁶May all who come to you
be glad and joyful.
May all who are thankful for your salvation
always say, "How great is the Lord!"

17I am weak and poor, O Lord,
but you have not forgotten me.
You are my savior and my God–
hurry to my aid!

## A PRAYER FOR FORGIVENESS

1Be merciful to me, O God,
because of your constant love.
Because of your great mercy
wipe away my sins!
2Wash away all my evil
and make me clean from my sin!

3I recognize my faults;
I am always conscious of my sins.
4I have sinned against you–only against you–
and done what you consider evil.
So you are right in judging me;
you are justified in condemning me.
5I have been evil from the day I was born;
from the time I was conceived, I have been sinful.

6Sincerity and truth are what you require;
fill my mind with your wisdom.
7Remove my sin, and I will be clean;
wash me, and I will be whiter than snow.
8Let me hear the sounds of joy and gladness;
and though you have crushed me and broken me,
I will be happy once again.
9Close your eyes to my sins
and wipe out all my evil.

10Create a pure heart in me, O God,
and put a new and loyal spirit in me.
11Do not banish me from your presence;
do not take your holy spirit away from me.
12Give me again the joy that comes from your salvation,
and make me willing to obey you.
13Then I will teach sinners your commands,
and they will turn back to you.

14Spare my life, O God, and save me,
and I will gladly proclaim your righteousness.
15Help me to speak, Lord,
and I will praise you.

16You do not want sacrifices,
or I would offer them;
you are not pleased with burnt offerings.
17My sacrifice is a humble spirit, O God;
you will not reject a humble and repentant heart.

[18]O God, be kind to Zion and help her;
rebuild the walls of Jerusalem.
[19]Then you will be pleased with proper sacrifices
and with our burnt offerings;
and bulls will be sacrificed on your altar.

## A PRAYER FOR SAFETY

PSALM 58 (59)

[1]Save me from my enemies, my God;
protect me from those who attack me!
[2]Save me from those evil people;
rescue me from those murderers!

[3]Look! They are waiting to kill me;
cruel people are gathering against me.
It is not because of any sin or wrong I have done,
[4]nor because of any fault of mine, O Lord,
that they hurry to their places.

[5]Rise, Lord God Almighty, and come to my aid;
see for yourself, God of Israel!
Wake up and punish the heathen;
show no mercy to evil traitors!

[6]They come back in the evening,
snarling like dogs as they go about the city.
[7]Listen to their insults and threats.
Their tongues are like swords in their mouths,
yet they think that no one hears them.

[8]But you laugh at them, Lord;
you mock all the heathen.
[9]I have confidence in your strength;
you are my refuge, O God.
[10]My God loves me and will come to me;
he will let me see my enemies defeated.

[11]Do not kill them, O God, or my people may forget.
Scatter them by your strength and defeat them,
O Lord, our protector.
[12]Sin is on their lips; all their words are sinful;
may they be caught in their pride!
Because they curse and lie,
[13]destroy them in your anger;
destroy them completely.
Then everyone will know that God rules in Israel,
that his rule extends over all the earth.

[14]My enemies come back in the evening,
snarling like dogs as they go about the city,
[15]like dogs roaming about for food
and growling if they do not find enough.

<sup>16</sup>But I will sing about your strength;
every morning I will sing aloud of your constant love.
You have been a refuge for me,
a shelter in my time of trouble.
<sup>17</sup>I will praise you, my defender.
My refuge is God,
the God who loves me.


## A PRAYER FOR HELP

*PSALM 85 (86)*

<sup>1</sup>Listen to me, Lord, and answer me,
for I am helpless and weak.
<sup>2</sup>Save me from death, because I am loyal to you;
save me, for I am your servant and I trust in you.

<sup>3</sup>You are my God, so be merciful to me;
I pray to you all day long.
<sup>4</sup>Make your servant glad, O Lord,
because my prayers go up to you.
<sup>5</sup>You are good to us and forgiving,
full of constant love for all who pray to you.

<sup>6</sup>Listen, Lord, to my prayer;
hear my cries for help.
<sup>7</sup>I call to you in times of trouble,
because you answer my prayers.

<sup>8</sup>There is no god like you, O Lord,
not one has done what you have done.
<sup>9</sup>All the nations that you have created
will come and bow down to you;
they will praise your greatness.
<sup>10</sup>You are mighty and do wonderful things;
you alone are God.

<sup>11</sup>Teach me, Lord, what you want me to do,
and I will obey you faithfully;
teach me to serve you with complete devotion.
<sup>12</sup>I will praise you with all my heart, O Lord my God;
I will proclaim your greatness forever.
<sup>13</sup>How great is your constant love for me!
You have saved me from the grave itself.
<sup>14</sup>Proud people are coming against me, O God;
a cruel gang is trying to kill me—
people who pay no attention to you.
<sup>15</sup>But you, O Lord, are a merciful and loving God,
always patient, always kind and faithful.
<sup>16</sup>Turn to me and have mercy on me;
strengthen me and save me,
because I serve you just as my mother did.

¹⁷Show me proof of your goodness, Lord;
those who hate me will be ashamed
when they see that you have given me
comfort and help.

## A CRY FOR HELP

¹Lord God, my savior, I cry out all day,
and at night I come before you.
²Hear my prayer;
listen to my cry for help!

³So many troubles have fallen on me
that I am close to death.
⁴I am like all others who are about to die;
all my strength is gone.
⁵I am abandoned among the dead;
I am like the slain lying in their graves,
those you have forgotten completely,
who are beyond your help.
⁶You have thrown me into the depths of the tomb,
into the darkest and deepest pit.
⁷Your anger lies heavy on me,
and I am crushed beneath its waves.

⁸You have caused my friends to abandon me;
you have made me repulsive to them.
I am closed in and cannot escape;
⁹my eyes are weak from suffering.
Lord, every day I call to you
and lift my hands to you in prayer.

¹⁰Do you perform miracles for the dead?
Do they rise up and praise you?
¹¹Is your constant love spoken of in the grave
or your faithfulness in the place of destruction?
¹²Are your miracles seen in that place of darkness
or your goodness in the land of the forgotten?

¹³Lord, I call to you for help;
every morning I pray to you.
¹⁴Why do you reject me, Lord?
Why do you turn away from me?
¹⁵Ever since I was young, I have suffered and been near death;
I am worn out from the burden of your punishments.
¹⁶Your furious anger crushes me;
your terrible attacks destroy me.
¹⁷All day long they surround me like a flood;
they close in on me from every side.
¹⁸You have made even my closest friends abandon me,
and darkness is my only companion.

## A SONG OF PRAISE

*PSALM 91 (92)*

¹How good it is to give thanks to you, O Lord,
to sing in your honor, O Most High God,
²to proclaim your constant love every morning
and your faithfulness every night,
³with the music of stringed instruments
and with melody on the harp.
⁴Your mighty deeds, O Lord, make me glad;
because of what you have done, I sing for joy.

⁵How great are your actions, Lord!
How deep are your thoughts!
⁶This is something a fool cannot know;
someone who is stupid cannot understand:
⁷the wicked may grow like weeds,
those who do wrong may prosper;
yet they will be totally destroyed,
⁸because you, Lord, are supreme forever.

⁹We know that your enemies will die,
and all the wicked will be defeated.
¹⁰You have made me as strong as a wild ox;
you have blessed me with happiness.
¹¹I have seen the defeat of my enemies
and heard the cries of the wicked.

¹²The righteous will flourish like palm trees;
they will grow like the cedars of Lebanon.
¹³They are like trees planted in the house of the Lord,
that flourish in the Temple of our God,
¹⁴that still bear fruit in old age
and are always green and strong.
¹⁵This shows that the Lord is just,
that there is no wrong in my protector.

## THE LOVE OF GOD

*PSALM 102 (103)*

¹Praise the Lord, my soul!
All my being, praise his holy name!
²Praise the Lord, my soul,
and do not forget how kind he is.
³He forgives all my sins
and heals all my diseases.
⁴He keeps me from the grave
and blesses me with love and mercy.
⁵He fills my life with good things,
so that I stay young and strong like an eagle.

⁶The Lord judges in favor of the oppressed
and gives them their rights.
⁷He revealed his plans to Moses

and let the people of Israel see his mighty deeds.
[8]The Lord is merciful and loving,
slow to become angry and full of constant love.
[9]He does not keep on rebuking;
he is not angry forever.
[10]He does not punish us as we deserve
or repay us according to our sins and wrongs.
[11]As high as the sky is above the earth,
so great is his love for those who honor him.
[12]As far as the east is from the west,
so far does he remove our sins from us.
[13]As a father is kind to his children,
so the Lord is kind to those who honor him.
[14]He knows what we are made of;
he remembers that we are dust.

[15]As for us, our life is like grass.
We grow and flourish like a wild flower;
[16]then the wind blows on it, and it is gone–
no one sees it again.
[17]But for those who honor the Lord, his love lasts forever,
and his goodness endures for all generations
[18]of those who are true to his covenant
and who faithfully obey his commands.

[19]The Lord placed his throne in heaven;
he is king over all.
[20]Praise the Lord, you strong and mighty angels,
who obey his commands,
who listen to what he says.
[21]Praise the Lord, all you heavenly powers,
you servants of his, who do his will!
[22]Praise the Lord, all his creatures
in all the places he rules.
Praise the Lord, my soul!

## IN PRAISE OF GOD'S GOODNESS

*PSALM 106 (107)*

[1]"Give thanks to the Lord,
because he is good;
his love is eternal!"
[2]Repeat these words in praise to the Lord,
all you whom he has saved.
He has rescued you from your enemies
[3]and has brought you back from foreign countries,
from east and west, from north and south.

[4]Some wandered in the trackless desert
and could not find their way to a city to live in.
[5]They were hungry and thirsty
and had given up all hope.

⁶Then in their trouble they called to the Lord,
and he saved them from their distress.
⁷He led them by a straight road
to a city where they could live.
⁸They must thank the Lord for his constant love,
for the wonderful things he did for them.
⁹He satisfies those who are thirsty
and fills the hungry with good things.

¹⁰Some were living in gloom and darkness,
prisoners suffering in chains,
¹¹because they had rebelled against the commands
of Almighty God
and had rejected his instructions.
¹²They were worn out from hard work;
they would fall down, and no one would help.
¹³Then in their trouble they called to the Lord,
and he saved them from their distress.
¹⁴He brought them out of their gloom and darkness
and broke their chains in pieces.
¹⁵They must thank the Lord for his constant love,
for the wonderful things he did for them.
¹⁶He breaks down doors of bronze
and smashes iron bars.

¹⁷Some were fools, suffering because of their sins
and because of their evil;
¹⁸they couldn't stand the sight of food
and were close to death.
¹⁹Then in their trouble they called to the Lord,
and he saved them from their distress.
²⁰He healed them with his command
and saved them from the grave.
²¹They must thank the Lord for his constant love,
for the wonderful things he did for them.
²²They must thank him with sacrifices,
and with songs of joy must tell all that he has done.

²³Some sailed over the ocean in ships,
earning their living on the seas.
²⁴They saw what the Lord can do,
his wonderful acts on the seas.
²⁵He commanded, and a mighty wind began to blow
and stirred up the waves.
²⁶The ships were lifted high in the air
and plunged down into the depths.
In such danger the sailors lost their courage;
²⁷they stumbled and staggered like drunks—
all their skill was useless.
²⁸Then in their trouble they called to the Lord,
and he saved them from their distress.
²⁹He calmed the raging storm,

and the waves became quiet.
³⁰They were glad because of the calm,
and he brought them safe to the port they wanted.
³¹They must thank the Lord for his constant love,
for the wonderful things he did for them.
³²They must proclaim his greatness
in the assembly of the people
and praise him before the council of the leaders.

³³The Lord made rivers dry up completely
and stopped springs from flowing.
³⁴He made rich soil become a salty wasteland
because of the wickedness of those who lived there.
³⁵He changed deserts into pools of water
and dry land into flowing springs.
³⁶He let hungry people settle there,
and they built a city to live in.
³⁷They sowed the fields and planted grapevines
and reaped an abundant harvest.
³⁸He blessed his people, and they had many children;
he kept their herds of cattle from decreasing.

³⁹When God's people were defeated and humiliated
by cruel oppression and suffering,
⁴⁰he showed contempt for their oppressors
and made them wander in trackless deserts.
⁴¹But he rescued the needy from their misery
and made their families increase like flocks.
⁴²The righteous see this and are glad,
but all the wicked are put to silence.

⁴³May those who are wise think about these things;
may they consider the Lord's constant love.

## SOMEONE SAVED FROM DEATH PRAISES GOD

*PSALM 114 (116)*

¹I love the Lord, because he hears me;
he listens to my prayers.
²He listens to me
every time I call to him.
³The danger of death was all around me;
the horrors of the grave closed in on me;
I was filled with fear and anxiety.
⁴Then I called to the Lord,
"I beg you, Lord, save me!"

⁵The Lord is merciful and good;
our God is compassionate.
⁶The Lord protects the helpless;
when I was in danger, he saved me.
⁷Be confident, my heart,
because the Lord has been good to me.

⁸The Lord saved me from death;
he stopped my tears
and kept me from defeat.
⁹And so I walk in the presence of the Lord
in the world of the living.

## THE LORD OUR PROTECTOR

*PSALM 120 (121)*

¹I look to the mountains;
where will my help come from?
²My help will come from the Lord,
who made heaven and earth.

³He will not let you fall;
your protector is always awake.

⁴The protector of Israel
never dozes or sleeps.
⁵The Lord will guard you;
he is by your side to protect you.
⁶The sun will not hurt you during the day,
nor the moon during the night.

⁷The Lord will protect you from all danger;
he will keep you safe.
⁸He will protect you as you come and go
now and forever.

## IN PRAISE OF GOD'S GOODNESS

*PSALM 126 (127)*

¹If the Lord does not build the house,
the work of the builders is useless;
if the Lord does not protect the city,
it does no good for the sentries to stand guard.
²It is useless to work so hard for a living,
getting up early and going to bed late.
For the Lord provides for those he loves,
while they are asleep.

³Children are a gift from the Lord;
they are a real blessing.
⁴The sons a man has when he is young
are like arrows in a soldier's hand.
⁵Happy is the man who has many such arrows.
He will never be defeated
when he meets his enemies in the place of judgment.

## A PRAYER FOR HELP

[1]From the depths of my despair
I call to you, Lord.
[2]Hear my cry, O Lord;
listen to my call for help!
[3]If you kept a record of our sins,
who could escape being condemned?
[4]But you forgive us,
so that we should stand in awe of you.

[5]I wait eagerly for the Lord's help,
and in his word I trust.
[6]I wait for the Lord
more eagerly than sentries wait for the dawn–
than sentries wait for the dawn.

[7]Israel, trust in the Lord,
because his love is constant
and he is always willing to save.
[8]He will save his people Israel
from all their sins.

## A PRAYER OF HUMBLE TRUST

[1]Lord, I have given up my pride
and turned away from my arrogance.
I am not concerned with great matters
or with subjects too difficult for me.
[2]Instead, I am content and at peace.
As a child lies quietly in its mother's arms,
so my heart is quiet within me.
[3]Israel, trust in the Lord
now and forever!

## IN PRAISE OF LIVING IN PEACE

[1]How wonderful it is, how pleasant,
for God's people to live together in harmony!
[2]It is like the precious anointing oil
running down from Aaron's head and beard,
down to the collar of his robes.
[3]It is like the dew on Mount Hermon,
falling on the hills of Zion.
That is where the Lord has promised his blessing–
life that never ends.

## GOD'S COMPLETE KNOWLEDGE AND CARE

*PSALM 138 (139)*

¹Lord, you have examined me and you know me.
²You know everything I do;
from far away you understand all my thoughts.
³You see me, whether I am working or resting;
you know all my actions.
⁴Even before I speak,
you already know what I will say.
⁵You are all around me on every side;
you protect me with your power.
⁶Your knowledge of me is too deep;
it is beyond my understanding.

⁷Where could I go to escape from you?
Where could I get away from your presence?
⁸If I went up to heaven, you would be there;
if I lay down in the world of the dead, you would be there.
⁹If I flew away beyond the east
or lived in the farthest place in the west,
¹⁰you would be there to lead me,
you would be there to help me.

¹¹I could ask the darkness to hide me
or the light around me to turn into night,
¹²but even darkness is not dark for you,
and the night is as bright as the day.
Darkness and light are the same to you.

¹³You created every part of me;
you put me together in my mother's womb.
¹⁴I praise you because you are to be feared;
all you do is strange and wonderful.
I know it with all my heart.
¹⁵When my bones were being formed,
carefully put together in my mother's womb,
when I was growing there in secret,
you knew that I was there–
¹⁶you saw me before I was born.
The days allotted to me
had all been recorded in your book,
before any of them ever began.
¹⁷O God, how difficult I find your thoughts;
how many of them there are!
¹⁸If I counted them, they would be more
than the grains of sand.
When I awake, I am still with you.

¹⁹O God, how I wish you would kill the wicked!
How I wish violent people would leave me alone!
²⁰They say wicked things about you;
they speak evil things against your name.
²¹O Lord, how I hate those who hate you!

How I despise those who rebel against you!
22I hate them with a total hatred;
I regard them as my enemies.

23Examine me, O God, and know my mind;
test me, and discover my thoughts.
24Find out if there is any evil in me
and guide me in the everlasting way.

### A CALL FOR THE UNIVERSE TO PRAISE GOD

*PSALM 148*

1Praise the Lord!

Praise the Lord from heaven,
you that live in the heights above.
2Praise him, all his angels,
all his heavenly armies.

3Praise him, sun and moon;
praise him, shining stars.
4Praise him, highest heavens,
and the waters above the sky.

5Let them all praise the name of the Lord!
He commanded, and they were created;
6by his command they were fixed in their places forever,
and they cannot disobey.

7Praise the Lord from the earth,
sea monsters and all ocean depths;
8lightning and hail, snow and clouds,
strong winds that obey his command.

9Praise him, hills and mountains,
fruit trees and forests;
10all animals, tame and wild,
reptiles and birds.

11Praise him, kings and all peoples,
princes and all other rulers;
12young women and young men,
old people and children too.

13Let them all praise the name of the Lord!
His name is greater than all others;
his glory is above earth and heaven.
14He made his nation strong,
so that all his people praise him—
the people of Israel, so dear to him.

Praise the Lord!

## THE LORD'S PRAYER

Our Father, who art in heaven,
hallowed be thy name;
thy kingdom come;
thy will be done
on earth as it is in heaven.

Give us this day
our daily bread;
and forgive us our trespasses
as we forgive those
who trespass against us;
and lead us not into temptation,
but deliver us from evil. Amen.

## HAIL MARY

Hail Mary, full of grace,
the Lord is with thee.
Blessed art thou among women
and blessed is the fruit of thy womb, Jesus.

Holy Mary, Mother of God,
pray for us sinners,
now and the hour of our death. Amen.

## CREED

I believe in God, the Father almighty,
creator of heaven and earth.
I believe in Jesus Christ, his only Son, our Lord.
He was conceived by the power of the Holy Spirit
and born of the Virgin Mary.
He suffered under Pontius Pilate,
was crucified, died, and was buried.
He descended to the dead.
On the third day he rose again.
He ascended into heaven,
and is seated at the right hand of the Father.
He will come again to judge the living and the dead.
I believe in the Holy Spirit, the holy catholic Church,
the communion of saints, the forgiveness of sins,
the resurrection of the body, and the life everlasting.

## MAGNIFICAT

My soul proclaims the greatness of the Lord,
my spirit exults in God my Saviour;
for he has looked with favour
on his lowly servant.

From this day all generations will call me blessed:
the Almighty has done great things for me,
and holy is his Name.

He has mercy on those who fear him
in every generation.
He has shown the strength of his arm,
he has scattered the proud in their conceit.

He has cast down the mighty from their thrones,
and has lifted up the lowly.
He has filled the hungry with good things,
and the rich he has sent away empty.

He has come to the help of his servant Israel
for he has remembered his promise of mercy,
the promise he made to our ancestors,
to Abraham and his children for ever.

## MAGNIFICAT

Magnificat
anima mea Dominum,
et exsultavit spiritus meus,
quia respexit humilitatem ancillæ suæ.
Ece enim ex hoc beatam me dicent omnes generationes.

Quia fecit mihi magna, qui potens est
et sanctum nomen eius,
et misericordia eius in progenies et progenies
timentibus eum.

Fecit potentiam in brachio suo,
dispersit superbos mente cordis sui ;
deposuit potentes de sede
et exaltavit humiles ;
esurientes implevit bonis
et divites dimisit inanes.

Suscepit Israel puerum suum,
recordatus misericordiæ
sicut locutus est ad patres nostros,
Abraham et semini eius in sæcula.

## SALVE REGINA

Hail, Holy Queen,
mother of mercy,
our life, our sweetness
and our hope.
To you do we cry,
poor banished children of Eve;
to you we send up our sighs,

Salve, Regina,
Mater misericordiæ,
vita, dulcedo
et spes nostra, salve !
Ad te clamamus,
exules filii Hevæ.
Ad te suspiramus,

mourning and weeping
in this valley of tears.
Turn then, most gracious advocate,
your eyes of mercy
upon us,
and after this, our exile,
show unto us
the blessed fruit of your womb,
Jesus.
O clement,
O loving,
O kind Virgin Mary.

gementes et flentes
in hac lacrymarum valle.
Eia ergo, advocata nostra,
illos tuos misericordes
oculos ad nos converte.
Et Jesum, benedictum,
fructum ventris tui,
nobis post
hoc exilium ostende.
O clemens,
o pia,
o dulcis Virgo Maria !

## ANGELUS

The angel of the Lord declared unto Mary,
and she conceived of the Holy Spirit.
*Hail Mary...*

Behold, the handmaid of the Lord;
be it done to me according to your word.
*Hail Mary...*

And the word was made flesh,
and dwelt among us.
*Hail Mary...*

Pray for us, O holy Mother of God;
that we may be made worthy of the promises of Christ.

Pour forth, we beseech you, O Lord, your grace into our hearts that we,
to whom the incarnation of your Son was made known by the message
of an angel, may by his passion and cross be brought to the glory of his
resurrection. We ask this through the same Christ, our Lord. Amen.

## VENI CREATOR

Come, Holy Spirit, Creator blest,
And in our hearts take up your rest;
Come with your grace and heavenly aid
To fill the hearts which you have made.

O Comforter, to you we cry,
The heavenly gift of God most High;
The fount of life and fire of love,
And sweet anointing from above.

To every sense your light impart,
And shed your love in every heart.
To our weak flesh your strength supply:
Unfailing courage from on high.

O grant that we through you may come
To know the Father and the Son,

And hold with firm, unchanging faith
That you are Spirit of them both.

Now let us praise Father and Son,
And Holy Spirit, with them one;
And may the Son on us bestow
The gifts that from the Spirit flow.

## ACT OF CONTRITION

My God,
I am sorry for my sins with all my heart.
In choosing to do wrong and failing to do good,
I have sinned against you
whom I should love above all things.

I firmly intend, with your help,
to do penance, to sin no more,
and to avoid whatever leads me to sin.

Our Saviour Jesus Christ suffered and died for us.
In his name, my God, have mercy.

## PRAYER OF ST. FRANCIS

Lord, make me an instrument of your peace.
Where there is hatred, let me sow love;
where there is injury, pardon;
where there is doubt, faith;
where there is despair, hope;
where there is darkness, light;
and where there is sadness, joy;

Divine Master,
grant that I may not so much seek
to be consoled as to console,
to be understood as to understand,
to be loved as to love.

For it is in giving that we receive,
in pardoning that we are pardoned,
and in dying that we are born to eternal life.

## PRAYER FOR THE VOCATIONS

Jesus, High Priest and Redeemer forever,
we beg you to call young men and women
to your service as priests and religious.
May they be inspired by the lives of dedicated priests,
Brothers and Sisters.
Give to parents the grace of generosity and trust
toward you and their children
so that their sons and daughters

may be helped to choose their vocation in life
with wisdom and freedom.

Lord, you told us that
"the harvest indeed is great but the laborers are few.
Pray, therefore, the Lord of the harvest
to send laborers into his harvest."
We ask that we may know and follow
the vocation to which you have called us.
We pray particularly for those called to serve as priests,
Brothers and Sisters;
those whom you have called,
those you are calling now,
and those you will call in the future.
May they be open and responsive to the call of serving your people.
We ask this through Christ, our Lord. Amen.

### PRAYER FOR POPE JOHN PAUL II

Lord, you have given us a pastor after your own heart.
From him, we have received your Word,
your mercy and your commandments.
We beg you to keep your hand lovingly on him.
Protect him, keep on giving him your strength and your zeal
To proclaim your Gospel throughout the world
So that all may have life.
Amen.

# ANSWERING
# THE CALL

88    ANSWERING THE CALL

# Sisters of the Assumption of the Blessed Virgin

As Sisters of the Assumption, with Jesus we are committed to live the Gospel. Listen to the reason why he sends us into the world: to reveal his love in an educational mission with a preference for youth, women and the poor.

From the past (1853) to the present, we have been gifted with the love of Jesus; we are happy to share it and to take it wherever his Spirit leads us. Approaching the year 2000, we are committed to being bearers of life in a communion without boundaries, concerned with living in solidarity with the oppressed and the destitute in our Mission centers in Canada, in the United States, in Japan, in Brazil, in Ecuador and in Haiti.

Our commitments are rooted in faith in the Divine Providence and enhanced with a Marian presence. Mary draws us to fullness of life and molds us to be symbols of hope.

Have you felt Jesus' gaze upon you? Is he calling you to follow in his footsteps? Do you hear the cries of youth, of women and of the poor who yearn for a better life? Are you impelled to respond to the challenge of sharing love and promoting hope in an educational Mission? Come, join us, and choose LIFE!

*Canada*
311, rue Saint-Jean-Baptiste
Nicolet (Québec) J3T 1H5
Canada
Tel.: (1) 819-293-4432
Fax: (1) 819-293-5754

*United States*
316, Lincoln Street
Worcester, MA
U.S.A.
Tel.: (1) 508-856-9448
Fax: (1) 508-853-0881

*Japan*
6-32, 2 Chôme Namiuchi
030 Aomori-Shi
Aomori-Ken - Japan
Tel.: (81) 177-41-0122
Fax: (81) 172-33-6618

*Ecuador*
calle Pedro Alvarado appt 57
Frente al Bloque Camarones
San Carlos Quitto
Ecuador

*Brazil*
Rua Guaraniaçu, 64
Ibura – U.R.2
51340-060 Recife
Brazil
Tel. / fax: (55) 81-475-1797

❀

# Sisters of the Good Shepherd of Québec

## Founded in 1850 by Marie-Josephte Fitzbach, Mother Mary of the Sacred Heart

If you want to know the Good Shepherd Sisters of Québec, come and see! Our Foundress, Marie-Josephte Fitzbach, was 43 when she founded our Institute in 1850, at the request of the Archbishop of Québec and the St. Vincent de Paul Society. At the time, she was a resident at the convent of the Sisters of Charity of Québec, where her two daughters were novices. Motivated solely by the love of God and the hope of leading to Jesus the women in moral distress who would be entrusted to her, she accepted to open a refuge for them. From the Heart of Jesus and the immaculate Heart of Mary, she drew the tenderness and goodness that marked her life. She founded our Congregation on the basis of contemplation and service.

Today, wherever we minister, we strive to relieve physical and moral distress, teach the truths of the faith and thereby touch hearts and lead them to Jesus the Good Shepherd. We invent the way to live that ministry of mercy and faith education in today's world, in search of justice, love and peace. Come, and you will see! You can reach us in:

**Canada**
General administration
2550, rue Marie-Fitzbach
Sainte-Foy (Québec) G1V 2J2
Canada
Tel.: (1) 418-656-0650
Fax: (1) 418-656-9737

**United States**
Provincial house
313 Seaside Avenue
Saco, ME 04072 U.S.A.
Tel.: (1) 207-283-3433
Fax: (1) 207-282-7376

**Lesotho**
Provincial house
P.O. Box 01165
Maseru West
Lesotho
Tel.: 266-31-2322
Fax: 266-31-0197

**Haiti**
Regional house
24, rue Bordes
Haiti
Tel.: (509) 84-5214
Fax: (509) 84-6451

**Brazil**
Casa Regional, S.C.I.M.
C.P. 236
59 001-970, Natal, RN
Brazil
Tel. / fax: (55) 84-205-4078

**Rwanda**
B.P. 888
Kigali
Rwanda
Tel. / fax: 250-8-4982

❋

# The Capuchins (o.f.m. Cap.)

The Capuchins, founded by Saint Francis of Assisi in the 13th century, make the Gospel their rule of life, following in the footsteps of Christ in his humility and poverty.

We are 12,000 friars (both priests and laymen) at work on all continents, striving to further the cause of peace, love, justice and fraternity.

Our simple life has its priorities: contemplation, fraternal life and ministerial commitment.

We endeavour to translate into our life the Prayer for Peace, signed by Francis:

"Lord, make me an instrument of your peace. Where there is hatred, let me sow love; where there is injury, pardon; where there is doubt, faith; where there is despair, hope; where there is darkness, light; and where there is sadness, joy."

*Canada*
Fraternité des Capucins
2610, rue Désormeaux
Montréal (Québec) H1L 4X5
Canada

Provincial house
2100 Jane Street
P.O. Box 520 Station A
Downsview (Ontario) M3M 3A8
Canada

Capucin Friary
53, Ettrick Crescent
Weston (Ontario) M9M 2K7
Canada

*France*
Fraternité des Capucins
32, rue Boissonnade
75014 Paris
France

*Italy*
General administration
Frati Cappuccini
Via Piemonte 70
00187 Roma
Italia

For the other countries, inquire locally.

❊

# THE CARMELITE ORDER

## A "HOLY MOUNTAIN" IMPLANTED ON EVERY CONTINENT

Land of saints, it bears fruit which remain: Theresa of Jesus (Avila), John of the Cross; and closer to us: Thérèse de l'Enfant-Jésus (Lisieux), Elisabeth of the Trinity, Edith Stein, Teresa de Los Andes, Raphael Kalinowski and many others.

You have felt in your heart the presence of Christ? You want to look further for him, taking with you all of humanity? Allow his love to burn in you and his Fire to take over the whole earth reaching the heart of the Church, and the hearts of all men.

A big family: Carmelite brothers and sisters, religious congregations, secular institutes, brotherhoods.

The Carmelite Order is present in 90 countries around the world.

❊

# SISTERS OF CHARITY OF MONTREAL ("GREY NUNS")

## FOUNDED IN MONTREAL (CANADA) IN 1737, BY MARGUERITE DUFROST DE LAJEMMERAIS, WIDOW D'YOUVILLE

We are a Congregation founded to make known the tenderness of God the Father for all people, especially the less fortunate. From across Canada, the United States and Latin America (Brazil, Colombia and Argentina), together we are summoned to be signs of hope and compassion in our broken world.

We freely choose to commit ourselves to live in communion with one another, respecting the richness of diversity in unity, striving to be credible and convincing witnesses. We assume co-responsibility for building the community, and we call forth the giftedness of each other in the service to the poor.

If from deep within you feel the desire to love Jesus and the poor, and wish to give your life to comfort those in need, come join us. You can come and see how we live, and if you have the required dispositions, you can help us accomplish so much more by using your God-given gifts.

For more information, write to:

***General administration***
138, rue Saint-Pierre
Montréal (Québec) H2Y 2l7
Canada

***Canadian provincial administrations***
1460, boul. Crémazie Est
Montréal (Québec) H2E 1A2
Canada

151, rue Despins
Saint-Boniface (Manitoba) R2H 0L7
Canada

55, rue Saint-Jean-Baptiste
Nicolet (Québec) J3T 1W4
Canada

9810-165 Street
Edmonton (Alberta) T5P 3S7
Canada

***American provincial administration***
10 Peiham Road
Lexington, MA 02173-5799
U.S.A.

***Latin America regional house***
Imas de Caridade
Rua Paulino Souza, 243
Monte Castelo
Sao Luis, MA - Brazil
65.035-480

❄

## SISTERS OF CHARITY OF OTTAWA

***Mission statement:*** We, the Sisters of Charity of Ottawa, a Congregation of consecrated women, daughters of Élisabeth Bruyère, stemming from Saint Marguerite d'Youville, bear witness to the compassionate love of the Father through our service of the poor and the teaching of the truth, according to the present needs of the people around us.

Guided by the Holy Spirit, trusting in the Providence and following Jesus and Mary, we remain available to answer the calls of the Church.

We have missions in the United States, in Africa (Lesotho, Republic of South Africa, Malawi, Zambia, Cameroon), in Japan, in Brazil, in Haiti and in Papua-New Guinea.

***Mother house***
9, rue Bruyère
Ottawa (Ontario) K1N 5C9
Canada

❄

# Sisters of Charity of Saint Louis

## Founded in 1803 by Marie-Louise-Élisabeth de Lamoignon Widow Molé de Champlâtreux (Mother Saint Louis)

We have been brought together in community to participate in the mission of Jesus Christ. Through our compassionate love, we strive for the healing of a world suffering from indifference, injustice, lack of love, dishonesty. Sustained and challenged by the Word of God and inflamed by the Holy Spirit, we seek to continue the evangelizing and liberating work of Christ. As an international community, we minister through various forms of education among the young, the sick, the poor, the disadvantaged. Aware of their concerns, we share, in a spirit of solidarity, the hope and forgiveness of Jesus and the tender love of the Father.

If you have a personal longing to make God better known and loved, if you wish to come closer to those who suffer in their hearts or bodies, Jesus may be calling you to mission with him. Please feel free to write to one of us.

*Canada*
Provincial House
6670, rue Saint-Louis-de-France
Lévis (Québec) G6V 1P3
Canada
Tel.: (1) 418-833-2101
Fax: (1) 418-833-4729

*France*
Mother House
18, place Théodore-Decker
56000 Vannes
France
Tel.: (33) 02-97-47-22-67
Fax: (33) 02-97-46-15-13

*Haiti*
Provincial House
360, av. J.-Brown
Bourdon – C.P. 437
Port-au-Prince
Tel. / Fax: (509) 45-57-28

*England*
Regional administration
58a Vauxhall Grove
London SW8 1TB
Great Britain
Tel.: (44) 171-793-0683
Fax: (44) 171-820-3880

Provincial Administration
3723 – 40 Street S.W.
Calgary (Alberta) T3E 3K4
Canada
Tel.: (1) 403-217-8803
Fax: (1) 403-217-4925

*Madagascar*
Regional House
Mandroseza, V.Q. 102A
Antananarivo
Madagascar
Tel.: 283-38

*Western Africa*
C.P. 152
Bamako
République du Mali
Tel. / Fax: (223) 22-03-12

*United States*
4907 South Catherine Street
Plattsburgh, New York 12901
U.S.A.
Tel.: (1) 518-563-7410
Fax: (1) 518-563-0383

❄

## ORDER OF SAINT CLARE (CLARES)

### PILGRIM WITH CLARE OF ASSISI

"Like pilgrims…"
(Clare, *Rule*)

Clare, pilgrim of the absolute:

– stable environment,
– deep-rooted life,
– forward looking.

"... never look backwards; rather, hurry forward with a light step, without falling on the stumbling blocks along your path... Go confidently, light-heartedly and joyously."

(Clare, *Letters*)

"I am the Way, the Truth, and the Life" (John 14:6).

"The disciples were on the way ... and Jesus went before them" (Mark 10:32).

"The young girl, the modern woman should find themselves in the splendid charism of Saint Clare, certainly hidden, certainly lacking any apparent exteriority, but how profound, how feminine."

John Paul II

***Canada***

Monastère Sainte-Claire
1200, ch. des Patriotes
Sorel (Québec)
Canada
Tel.: (1) 514-742-1171
Fax: (1) 514-742-1645

Monastère Sainte-Claire
7, rue Pelletier
Rivière-du-Loup (Québec)
Canada
Tel.: (1) 418-862-6300
Fax: (1) 418-862-0816

❄

## CLERICS OF SAINT VIATOR

### TO ANNOUNCE JESUS CHRIST AND HIS GOSPEL, AND THUS TO GIVE BIRTH TO COMMUNITIES WHERE FAITH IS LIVED AND CELEBRATED.

Such is the mission of the Viator communities. They are made up of fathers, brothers and associated laymen at the service of the local Churches, with a preference for the youth and the underpriviledged.

Louis Querbes (1793-1859) is their founder, and Viator, a reader of the Church of Lyon (4th century), their patron saint.

The members of the Saint Viator family, about a thousand strong, are present in thirteen countries, on four continents. Here are some addresses where you can join them.

**Canada**
Provincial secretariat
450, av. Querbes
Outremont (Québec) H2V 3W5
Canada

**Haiti**
Maison des Clercs de Saint-Viateur
C.P. 1408
Port-au-Prince
Haiti

**France**
Maison des Clercs de Saint-Viateur
3, rue Louis-Querbes
69390 Vourles
France

**Ivory Coast**
Maison des Clercs de Saint-Viateur
01 B.P. 1191
Bouaké 01
Ivory Coast

❄

# CONGREGATION OF HOLY CROSS

### "EVANGELICAL WORKERS TO BUILD A BETTER WORLD"

Founded in France by Father Basile Moreau in 1847, the Congregation of Holy Cross is an international religious family composed of sisters, brothers and priests.

"As disciples of Jesus, we stand side by side with all people. Thus, wherever the congregation sends us we go as educators of the faith to those whose lot we share, supporting men and women of grace and goodwill everywhere in their efforts to form communities of the coming kingdom." (Constitution 2, *Mission,* no.12)

Our apostolic involvement, by which we are very often called to answer the most urgent needs, stems from a strong spiritual life. We are constantly striving to "clothe ourselves in Christ", according to the expression used by Saint Paul, so that our words and our deeds foster unity and hope among human beings.

Are you interested in our mission? Do you want to join us? Then get in touch with us at the following addresses:

**Canada**
Raymond Gourde, c.s.c.
Oratoire Saint-Joseph
3800, ch. Queen Mary
Montréal (Québec) H3V 1H6
Canada
Tel.: (1) 514-341-7535
Fax: (1) 514-344-9911

Robert P. McInroy, c.s.c.
23 York Street
St. Catharines, Ontario L2R 6B7
Canada
Tel.: (1) 905-641-5749
Fax: (1) 905-641-0810

**Haiti**
Firto Régis, c.s.c.
Résidence Sainte-Croix
167, av. Jean-Paul II, C.P. 1230
Port-au-Prince
Haiti
Tel.: (509) 45-5838
Fax: (509) 45-4372

❊

# SISTERS OF THE CONGREGATION OF NOTRE-DAME

### FOUNDED IN THE 17th CENTURY IN MONTREAL (CANADA), BY SAINT MARGUERITE BOURGEOYS, NATIVE OF TROYES (FRANCE)

Like Mary who, carrying Jesus, "went with haste" to visit her cousin Elizabeth (Lk 1:39-56), we journey to bring the Good News of Jesus Christ to our brothers and sisters. It is as educators that we commit ourselves to different areas of ministry, working particularly with the impoverished, the excluded and the oppressed. We collaborate with other groups, lay or religious, and give special attention to youth, women and families.

If you are drawn to a spirituality of the Visitation and you hear a call to serve God in apostolic community life, please do not hesitate to contact us.

## *Canada*
Mother House
4873, av. Westmount
Montréal (Québec) H3Y 1X9
Canada
Tel.: (1) 514-489-8113
Fax: (1) 514-489-0014


Provincial House
56 Gill Court
P.O. Box 219
Pictou (Nova Scotia) B0K 1H0
Canada
Tel.: (1) 902-485-5996
Fax: (1) 902-485-4340

## *United States*
Provincial House
223 West Mountain Road
Ridgefield, CT 06877
Tel.: (1) 203-438-5282
Fax: (1) 203-438-3150


## *Central America*
Regional house
Apdo 428
11101 Tegucigalpa, F.M.
Honduras
Tel.: 504-32-3261
Fax: 504-35-8301

Provincial House
2810 Baycrest Drive
Ottawa (Ontario) K1V 7P7
Canada
Tel.: (1) 613-731-5041
Fax: (1) 613-731-5487


## *France*
Maison Notre-Dame en l'Isle
10, rue de l'Isle
10 000 Troyes
France
Tel. / fax: (33) 3-25-80-09-57


## *Japan*
Provincial House
3-55-1 Shimoishihara
Chofu-Shi
Tokyo 182
Tel.: (81) 424-82-8947
Fax: (81) 424-89-1793


## *Africa*
Douvangar Residence
C.P. 281
Maroua
Cameroon
Tel.: 237-29-10-52
Fax: 237-29-22-44 (Procure de
                    Maroua)

❊

## Dominican Missionary Adorers

### Founded in Beauport (Québec) in 1945 by Julienne Dallaire (Mother Julienne of the Rosary, o.p.)

Fascinated by the love by which Jesus gives himself to us in the Eucharist, we are consecrated to his Eucharistic Heart and to his mission of giving to the Father worshipers in spirit and in truth (cf. John 4:23). In the footsteps of St. Dominic, we want to guide our lives with the light of the Word of God, to contemplate our Savior by prayer and study, to proclaim the Truth through deeds and words. Assembled to live a fraternal life in Christ, together we offer the world to God and offer God to our world in search of love and of real meaning. Our missionary thrust encompasses the whole world. Faith education, formation and animation of the people of God in eucharistic life and spirituality, teaching, works of charity, such are the many forms of apostolate by which we proclaim the Gospel of the last Supper and make visible the love of the One who loves us "to the end" (John 13:1).

Like the Samaritan woman, you have a thirst to know the "gift of God". Like Dominic, your heart is filled with the great desire to proclaim truth. Like Jesus, "through him, with him and in him", you want to offer your life to God and to your brothers and sisters of the entire world. Listen to Jesus who invites you to share his life, his prayer and his mission of love. In order to better discern your vocation, you may contact us.

*Canada*
131, rue des Dominicaines
Beauport (Québec) G1E 6S8
Canada
Tel.: (1) 418-661-9221
Fax: (1) 418-663-1226

4613-47th Avenue
St. Paul (Alberta) T0A 3A3
Canada
Tel. / fax: (1) 403-645-6736

*Peru*
Blasco Nunez de Vela #528
El Carmen, Comas
Lima 7 Peru
Tel./ fax: (51) 1-541-0196

*Haiti*
C.P. 67
Cap-Haïtien
Haiti
Tel. / fax: (509)-62-0679

❋

## Dominicans of the Trinity

### Founded in 1887 by Philomène Labrecque (Mother Mary of the Charity) in Trois-Rivières (Québec) Canada

Members of the great Dominican Family, we work in service of the Church with priests, women, youth, and the sick and underprivileged.

Our charism: to be a reflection of the mercy of the Father.

The Word of God contemplated is prayed, celebrated, experienced, shared and proclaimed in the heart of everyday living.

(Addresses on next page.)

**Canada**
S. Denise Favreau, o.p.
2300, terrasse Mercure
Montréal (Québec) H2H 1P1
Canada
Tel.: (1) 514-524-8172 / 514-521-7984
Fax: (1) 514-522-6897

**Manila**
S. Constancia Pardillo, o.p.
Espana St. Sampaloc
1008 Manila
Philippines
Tel.: (63) 2-732-0846
Fax: (63) 2-731-3140

**Philippines**
S. Nieves Castro, o.p.
P.O. Box 80140
8000 Davao City
Philippines
Tel.: (63) 82-221-1838
Fax: (63) 82-221-5405

**Peru**
S. Edel. Penanueva, o.p.
Casilla 51
Chosica, Lima 15
Peru
Tel.: (51) 1-361-80-16
Fax: (51) 1-361-83-42

❈

# SISTERS OF THE INFANT JESUS OF CHAUFFAILLES

Our congregation was born in France in September 1859, in a place called Chauffailles. As circumstances would have it, the Sisters – Les Sœurs de l'Enfant-Jésus – came to the North Shore, the land of the poet Gilles Vigneault, in 1912, and arrived in Rivière-du-Loup in 1917.

Today, our family tree extends from France to Canada with establishments in Japan, in the Dominican Republic and in Chad. In Canada, we serve in the dioceses of Québec, Rimouski, La Pocatière and Ottawa.

Our foundress, Reine Antier, left us with a legacy for which we are proud. By our presence in today's world, we attempt to make known the Lord's love for all his children, no matter what their conditions in life may be. The way Reine Antier tried to live the teachings of the Gospel is what each member of the Congregation begins to feel when called by God; this call is nothing less than the mystery of the love of God become flesh as a child of Mary: it is the great mystery of the Incarnation.

We are open to all the requests that the Church makes to us through our bishops. That is why our sisters are found in different fields of endeavor: teaching both children and adults, caring for the sick and the elderly, helping the dispossessed whatever their needs. Our sisters are also found doing pastoral work in schools and in parishes.

However, there is a shadow on the horizon: there are many requests for help but fewer sisters to take on the workload; the needs are not being met with. So should you feel a call somewhere in your heart, take the time to think about it. You may find peace and happiness with us...

**France**
Mother house
27, rue du Huit-Mai
71170 Chauffailles
France
Tel.: (33) 3-85-26-02-14

General administration
2 bis, rue du Chalet
93370 Montfermeil
France
Tel.: (33) 1-43-32-44-73
Fax: (33) 1-43-32-51-74

*Japan*
Provincial house
Sister Matsuo Kyoko, superior
1/37 Nigawa Takadai, 2 Chôme
Takarazuka-Shi
Hyogo-Ken
Japan
Tel.: (81) 798-52-0174
Fax: (81) 798-51-7007

*Canada*
Provincial house
60, rue Saint-Henri
C.P. 820
Rivière-du-Loup (Québec)
G5R 3Z5
Canada
Tel.: (1) 418-862-3087
Fax: (1) 418-862-1970

*Dominican Republic*
Calle Duarte, # 104
Miches
Republica Dominicana
Tel.: 809-553-5722
Fax: 809-553-5252

*Chad*
Centre d'accueil de Kabalaye
Sister Lucille Morin, r.e.j.
B.P. 456
N'Djamena
Chad
Tel.: 235-51-82-48
Fax: 235-51-28-60

❊

# CONGREGATION OF JESUS AND MARY (THE EUDISTS)

The Eudists gather priests, deacons and lay people into a community, so that they can share their experience, their prayer and their calling.

In the midst of the world, true to their mission, the Eudists are involved in evangelizing the People of God and in training good workers of the Gospel. We aim at the renewal of faith through many diverse actions: giving witness by our life, prayer, preaching, faith education, being close to the youth, realizing various pastoral tasks. We also take special care in training and accompanying those who commit themselves to the service of evangelization.

The Eudists believe in you who are young, in your capacity of being and of doing. Today, we invite you. You could be among those the Lord calls to build a civilization of love where justice and tenderness walk hand in hand. If you want to know us better, come!

*North America*
Provincial house
6125, 1ʳᵉ Avenue
Charlesbourg (Québec) G1H 2V9
Canada
Tel.: (1) 418-626-6494
Fax: (1) 418-628-8774

*Colombia*
Provincial house
Transv. Nº 127 A – 73
Apdo aereo 100 997
Santa Fe de Bogota
Colombia
Tel.: (57) 1-626-55-15
Fax: (57) 1-258-31-10

*France*
Provincial house
1, rue Jean-Dolent
75014 Paris
France
Tel.: (33) 1-44-08-70-10
Fax: (33) 1-47-07-26-74

*Venezuela*
Provincial house
Apdo 80 510
Caracas 1080-A-80.510
Venezuela
Tel.: (58)-2-93-03-13
Fax: (58)-2-242-25-27

❋

# Daughters of Mary of the Assumption

## Founded in 1922 in Campbellton, New Brunswick, Canada, by L.-J.-Arthur Melanson, pastor

We, the Daughters of Mary of the Assumption, participate in the apostolic mission of the Church through all forms of Christian education for the young and the adults. All sisters are part of the mission of the Institute, each one according to her own gifts and capacity. Wherever we work, be it in Canada, in the Philippines or in Honduras, we are called to manifest our preferential option for the poor.

As members of a marian congregation, we honor Mary as the incomparable woman who gave Life to the world. From her, we learn to journey in faith and to become messengers of joy and hope through our daily commitment.

If you are interested in our life project and in the mission entrusted to us, please write to us for more information.

**Canada**
General administration
502, rue Vanier
C.P. 37
Campbellton (New Brunswick) E3N 3G1
Canada

**Philippines**
Assumption Sisters Regional House
P.O. Box 612
8100 Tagum
Davao Province
Philippines

**Honduras**
Hijas de Maria de la Assuncion
Casa Cural
C.P. 12112
Taulabé (Comayagua)
Honduras

❋

# Sisters of Mary of the Presentation

Following Christ the Servant, the Sisters of Mary of the Presentation devote themselves to serve their sisters and brothers as witnesses of the Kingdom of God in France, Belgium, Canada, the United States and Cameroon.

**France**
General Administration
27, rue de la Barrière
B.P. 31
22250 Broons
France
Tel.: (33) 02-96-84-62-31

**Belgium**
Dr Haubenlaan
3630 Maasmechelen
Belgium
Tel.: (32) 89-76-44-04

*Canada*
1171, rue Alexis-Simard
La Baie (Québec) G7B 2K5
Canada
Tel.: (1) 418-544-8203

*Africa*
B.P. 77
Batouri
Cameroon
Tel.: 237-26-22-56

*United States*
Maryvale 11550 River Road
Valley City
North Dakota 58072-9620
U.S.A.
Tel.: (1) 701-845-2864

❊

# FRANCISCAN MISSIONARIES OF MARY

At the service of the universal mission, we are more than 8,200 religious from 72 nationalities working in 77 countries on the five continents. The Eucharist, the center of our life, arouses and strengthens our missionary enthusiasm. From the Virgin Mary we learn to love, realizing our vocation as women by giving ourselves so that the life of others may develop. Following in the footsteps of St. Francis of Assisi, ready to go everywhere and to everyone, we make ourselves available, open to receive as well as to give.

You who seek God's plan for your life, would you like to be a messenger of the Good News? Here are some addresses for further information:

*Italy*
General administration
Via Giusti 12
00185 Rome
Italia
Tel.: (39) 6-70-45-35-55

*Canada*
Provincial house
145, ch. Presland
Ottawa (Ontario) K1K 2C1
Canada
Tel.: (1) 613-749-0848

Local residence
80, rue Laurier Est
Montréal (Québec) H2T 1E2
Canada
Tel.: (1) 514-279-7311

❊

# RELIGIOUS HOSPITALLERS OF SAINT JOSEPH (R.H.S.J.)

### FOUNDED BY JÉRÔME LE ROYER DE LA DAUVERSIÈRE
### IN 1636, IN LA FLÈCHE (FRANCE)

*Initial inspiration:* On the Feast of the Purification, February 2, 1630, Jérôme le Royer de la Dauversière had a spiritual experience. He was 33 years old and the grace received opened up new possibilities, leading him to establish a religious congregation. In 1635, he began to nurture a missionary project for Montreal. From that time on, the R.H.S.J. are called to live the liberty of the children of God as women of faith, incarnating the tender compassion of Christ especially among the poor, the sick and the most needy.

***To this day...*** Our mission in the Church as R.H.S.J. according to the charism and spiritual heritage transmitted by our founder, Jérôme le Royer and Marie de la Ferre, co-foundress, is to witness God's love which unites and frees. We are called to live this mission with men and women in today's world.

A challenge to meet... "together, look at persons beyond their differences to build unity and liberty" wherever we are: France, Canada, United States, Peru, Dominican Republic and Mexico.

Would you like more information? Contact us at the following addresses:

### *Canada*
2450, ch. de la Côte Sainte-Catherine
Montréal (Québec) H3T 1B1
Canada
Tel.: (1) 514-735-6585
Fax: (1) 514-735-6588

12144, rue Vallée-Lourdes
Bathurst (New Brunswick) E2A 4R9
Canada
Tel.: (1) 506-547-8322
Fax: (1) 506-547-8321

### *United States*
101 College Parkway
Colchester, Vermont 05446
U.S.A.
Tel.: (1) 802-655-1160
Fax: (1) 802-654-1458

### *Peru*
Apartado 130067
Serpost - La Victoria
Lima 13
Peru
Tel.: (51) 12-24-03-82
Fax: (51) 12-25-27-37

### *Mexico*
Apartado Postal 124
C.P. 56600
Chalco
Tel.: (52) 5-975-30-45

16 Manitou Crescent East
Kingston (Ontario) K7N 1B2
Canada
Tel.: (1) 613-389-0535
Fax: (1) 613-384-6978

### *France*
12, rue Dunant
72200 La Flèche
France
Tel.: (33) 02-43-45-25-85
Fax: (33) 02-43-94-68-42

644, Langlade Road
Antigo, Wisconsin 54409
U.S.A.
Tel. / fax: (1) 715-623-4615

### *Republica Dominicana*
Religiosas Hospitalarias
                    de San Jose
San Jose de Ocoa
Republica Dominicana
Tel.: 809-558-2434
Fax: 809-558-2837

❄

# RELIGIOUS OF JESUS AND MARY

### CONGREGATION FOUNDED IN 1818 IN LYON, FRANCE, BY CLAUDINE THÉVENET
### (CANONIZED BY POPE JOHN PAUL II ON MARCH 21, 1993)

Claudine's ardent charity urged her to devote herself to the education of the young, especially the less fortunate. For 180 years, the daughters of Claudine have travelled the world over, to spread the fire which quickened the heart of their foundress: "to make known God's active goodness."

In 25 countries, from France to India, from Rome to Lebanon, from Spain to Mexico and Cuba, from Canada to Africa, from Latin America to Eastern Europe, the Religious of Jesus-Mary find in the Eucharist the zeal that animates their apostolic work.

On March 20, 1993, the Beatification of one of their spiritual daughters, Dina Bélanger, a young Canadian nun who died in 1929 at the age of 32, confirmed the way chosen by Claudine. An artist and mystic, Dina would have liked "to travel the world to consume it in the infinite flames of the Sacred Heart."

*Italy*
Religiose di Gesù-Maria
Via Nomentana, 325
00162 Roma
Italia
Tel.: (39) 6 841-7666

*Canada*
Religieuses de Jésus-Marie
2049, ch. Saint-Louis
Sillery (Québec)
Canada
Tel.: (1) 418-687-9260

*Mexico*
Religiosas de Jesus-Maria
Cerrada Guillermo Prieto No 13
Huixquilucan, Estado de Mexico
Mexico
Tel.: (52) 5-812-4982

*France*
Religieuses de Jésus-Marie
2, place de Fourvière
69005 Lyon
France
Tel.: (33) 4-78-25-11-66

*Spain*
Religiosas de Jesus-Maria
Pso. San Gervasio, 15
08022 Barcelona
Spain
Tel.: (34) 3-211-0210

*United States*
Religious of Jesus and Mary
3706 Rhode Island Avenue
Mt Rainier, MD 29712-2009
U.S.A.
Tel.: (1) 301-277-3594

❊

# THE MARIST BROTHERS

The Marist Brothers were founded in 1817 by Marcellin Champagnat for the purpose of giving Christian education to the youth of France. The Congregation is now established in 70 countries around the world.

The Marist Brothers
7141, av. Royale
Château-Richer (Québec) G0A 1N0
Canada
Tel.: (1) 418-824-4215 — Fax: (1) 418-824-4128

❊

# MISSIONARIES OF AFRICA (WHITE FATHERS)

A Call to Missionary Life!

The Missionaries of Africa (White Fathers) are deeply involved with the peoples and Churches in Africa. Needs are many. Hence, we dare propose to all young people different types of commitments. If you feel called to missionary life and would like to know more about it, please get in touch with us.

*Canada*
Missionnaires d'Afrique
Pères Blancs
11100, boul. de l'Acadie
Montréal (Québec) H3M 2S8
Canada
Tel.: (1) 514-331-3520
Fax: (1) 514-331-2976

*France*
Missionnaires d'Afrique
Pères Blancs
5, rue Roger-Verlomme
75003 Paris
France
Tel.: (33) 1-42-71-06-70
Fax: (33) 1-48-04-39-67

*Spain*
Misioneros de Africa
Padres Blancos
c/Menorca 3 bajo
28009 Madrid
Spain
Tel.: (34) 1-574-400
Fax: (34) 1-504 2717

*Great Britain*
Missionaries of Africa
White Fathers
42 Stormont Road
London N6 4NP
Great Britain
Tel.: (44) 181-340-5036
Fax: (44) 181-347-8147

❊

# MISSIONARY SISTERS OF CHRIST THE KING

### FOUNDED IN GASPÉ IN 1928, BY FRÉDÉRICA GIROUX (SISTER MARY OF THE SACRED HEART)

Mother Frédérica Giroux wished the members of the Missionary Sisters of Christ the King to be women consecrated to God: by a life of prayer in the Church, by the proclamation of the Good News, by a life authentically lived and inspired by the spirituality of St. Ignatius of Loyola.

Are you willing to promote, defend and sustain life? Are you willing to seek ways to ensure the quality of life of your sisters and brothers? You can do this in countries throughout the world where the Missionary Sisters of Christ the King are working today: Canada, Haiti, Japan, South Korea, Ivory Coast, Chad and the Democratic Republic of Congo (Zaire).

To realize your dream, write to us:

*Canada*
4730, boul. Lévesque Ouest
Chomedy, Laval (Québec) H7W 2R4
Canada
Tel.: (1) 514-687-2100
Fax: (1) 514-687-2388

*Zaire*
B.P. 289 Mbujimayi
Kasaï Oriental
Zaire

**Japan**
4-10-26 Honcho
Hoya-shi, Tokyo-to 202
Japan
Tel.: (81) 424-65-8620
Fax: (81) 424-67-1624

**Ivory Coast**
Mission de Sinfra
B.P. 62, Sinfra
Ivory Coast
Tel.: 225-68-0016
Fax: 225-68-0064

**Haiti**
rue Debussy, Turgeau,
C.P. 1420
Port-au-Prince
Haiti
Tel. / fax: (509)-45-4706

❊

# MISSIONARY SISTERS OF THE IMMACULATE CONCEPTION

### FIRST CANADIAN MISSIONARY INSTITUTE FOUNDED IN 1902 BY DÉLIA TÉTREAULT (MOTHER MARY OF THE HOLY SPIRIT), BORN IN MARIEVILLE (QUÉBEC)

Our Institute gathers nearly 800 sisters working in 13 countries: Canada, Bolivia, Chile, Peru, Haiti, Cuba, Malawi, Zambia, Madagascar, Hong Kong, Taiwan, Japan, the Philippines.

Women of different nationalities, gathered by the same Call in fraternal communities, engaged in various ministries according to local Church needs.

Our spirituality is based in Marian and missionary thanksgiving. "The principal raison d'être of our Institute is really thanksgiving: may our life be a perpetual song of gratefulness..." (D.T.)

"Following the example of Mary, we will have to cross mountains and valleys to help our neighbour..." "Mary: love her and make people love her..." (D.T.)

"God gave us everything, even his only Son. What better way of paying him back than to give him children who will sing his goodness throughout the centuries..." (D.T.)

Since the remote days of continental China, missionaries have traveled on the roads of the world, answering all calls: for education, care of the sick, advancement of women, social work, etc. Deep faith, which involves the whole being, is the springboard of their missionary impetus. Simplicity, fraternal welcoming, joy, gratefulness, such is the climate in which the M.I.C. life is being built, in the quest of God's will and the building of his Kingdom of justice and peace.

As Délia, you want God to be known and loved, you want to build fraternity, you have a heart as wide as the world, you want to join in our M.I.C. work and spirit?

Here is where you can join us:

(Addresses on next page.)

## Canada

M.I.C. Mother House
314, chemin Sainte-Catherine
Outremont (Québec) H2V 2B4
Canada
Tel.: (1) 514-495-1551

1060, av. du Parc
Québec (Québec) G1S 2W7
Canada
Tel.: (1) 418-687-0520

121, av. Maplewood
Outremont (Québec) H2V 2M2
Canada
Tel.: (1) 514-274-5691

2950 Prince Edward St.
Vancouver, BC V5T 3N3
Canada
Tel.: (1) 604-874-9371

## Africa

Provincial House
P.O. Box 47
Mzimba
Malawi

## South America

Casa Provincial
Francisco de Orellana 338
Lima 5
Peru

## Cuba

Calle 33, No 3409 – Entre 34 y 36
Playa
Ciudad de la Habana
Cuba 12100

## Haiti

Provincial House (Delmas)
C.P. 1085
Port-au-Prince
Haiti

## Hong Kong

Provincial House
Mount Good Hope
381 Jat's Incline
Kowloon
Hong Kong

## Japan

Provincial House
8-13-16 Fukazawa, Setagaya Ku
Tokyo 158
Japan

## Madagascar

Provincial House
Lot II-J-4 bis, Ivandry
Antananarivo
Madagascar 101

## Philippines

Provincial House
P.O. Box 468, 1502 Greenhills
Metro Manila
Philippines

## Taiwan

Provincial House
30, Lane 148
Fu Hsing South Road, Section 2
Taipei 106
Taiwan

❀

## COMPANY OF MARY (MONTFORT FATHERS)

 Saint Louis-Marie Grignion de Montfort (1673-1716) was foremost and above all a man who was inhabited by the unique desire of Jesus Christ, "Eternal Wisdom made flesh". In his own personal experience as in his pastoral work, Montfort discovered in Mary, Mother of Jesus and first disciple, the perfect "spiritual environment" in which God can take root and grow in a human heart. It is through Mary's faith that Christ became part of this world; it is also through her that our world can open itself to God.

As a young priest, Montfort dreamed of missionaries that would know no frontiers, that would be "as free as the clouds, pushed by the breath of the Spirit", ready to go where needed and bring the Good News of Jesus Christ to all people, in a language relevant to modern man. The Montfort Fathers are present in over 30 countries (U.S.A., Canada, France, England, India, etc.)

To reach us:

*France*
Père Pierre Bonhommeau
52, rue Beaunier
75014 Paris
France
Tel.: (33) 1-45-40-50-56
Fax: (33) 1-45-40-74-61

*Canada*
Père Georges Madore
6455, av. Louis-Riel
Montréal (Québec) H1M 1P1
Canada
Tel.: (1) 514-253-8356
Fax: (1) 514-253-4300

❊

## THE NEWMAN CENTRE

A Catholic Mission at the University of Toronto, this Centre is born of the dream of John Henry Cardinal Newman of establishing a Catholic university in which theology, the arts and sciences would all be taught in dialogue with one another. Hosting a wealth of life and various activities (prayer group, groups of study and reflection on faith, ecumenism, social issues, etc.) the Newman Centre welcomes and forms lay people and seminarists for service in the Church.

The Newman Centre
89 St. George St.
Toronto (Ontario) M5S 2E8
Canada
Tel.: (1) 416-979-2468
Fax: (1) 416-596-6920

❊

## Sisters of the Good Shepherd

### Founded by Saint Marie-Euphrasie (Rose-Virginie Pelletier) in 1835

We, Sisters of the Good Shepherd of the six continents, are called to answer the needs of a new humanity in which a great diversity of cultures, ways of thinking and aspirations are evolving. Following Jesus the Good Shepherd, we have been called upon and sent to reveal the merciful love of the Father to those who feel rejected, hurt by sin and its consequences – especially girls and women.

Called to an active or a contemplative life, we believe that where the Love of Jesus the Good Shepherd is personally experimented, absorbed and shared, a climate of Joy and Hope is created among us and makes our mission significant to the world.

***Italy***
General administration
Via Raffaello Sardielle, 20
001654 Roma
Italia
Tel.: (39) 6-66-41-85-45

***France***
Mother house
3, rue Brault
49045 Angers Cédex 01
France
Tel.: (33) 2-41-71-12-80

***Canada***
Provincial house
9465, boul. Gouin Ouest
Pierrefonds (Québec) H8Y 1T2
Canada
Tel.: (1) 514-684-6680

Provincial house
25 Good Shepherd Court
Toronto (Ontario) M6B 4E7
Canada
Tel.: (1) 416-785-4554

❄

## Sisters of Our Lady of the Holy Rosary

The Institute, formerly known as the Sisters of Little Schools, was founded in Rimouski (Québec) in 1874. Called to manifest the tender and loving care of Jesus and Mary, Élisabeth Turgeon founded this Institute to respond to an urgent need of the area: the instruction and Christian education of the youth. Today, the sisters still pursue their mission in Canada, the United States, Honduras, Peru and Guatemala.

If you would like to know more about this Congregation, please communicate with the Superior General at the following address:

Sisters of Notre Dame of the Holy Rosary
375, rue Lasalle
Rimouski (Québec) G5L 3V6
Canada
Tel.: (1) 418-723-5329

❄

# MISSIONARY OBLATES OF MARY IMMACULATE

The Oblates of Mary Immaculate are missionaries in 68 countries. Their ideal is the evangelization of the poor. This ideal can be realized by rehabilitating drug addicts, by caring for victims of AIDS, by planning for inexpensive housing, by caring for refugees and migrants, as well as by re-evangelizing those who have wandered away from faith.

The adventures of this army of five thousand men began with Eugène de Mazenod in 1816. He founded a community of priests devoted to missions for evangelizing rural populations. After twenty-five years of intensive work in France, he sent his first missionaries to Canada. Shortly thereafter, missionaries were sent to Sri Lanka and Southern Africa. This was the beginning of the Oblate epic that was to continue amid the ice of the North Pole and in the heat of the tropics, in Christian, Moslem and Buddhist countries.

Eugène de Mazenod was canonized on December 3, 1995. This unique event, a time of communion with the Church of heaven and earth, brings us closer to our Founder. With ever more enthusiasm, Oblates and Oblate associates throughout the world are called to fully incarnate the charism received through St. Eugene. May God continue to bless us as we move into the next century.

For more information, you can reach us at the following addresses:

*Canada*

Fraternité Nazareth
2585, av. Letourneux
Montréal (Québec) H1V 2P3
Canada
Tel.: (1) 514-254-6257
Fax: (1) 514-254-6605

Résidence de Mazenod
455, boul. Père-Lelièvre
Ville de Vanier (Québec) G1M 1M9
Canada
Tel.: (1) 418-683-0806
Fax: (1) 418-681-6510

✺

# OBLATES OF THE VIRGIN MARY

We are known by our apostolic dynamism and our zeal for the New Evangelization, our concern for the advancement of the person, our respect for the Church's teaching, our closeness to the world of culture.

Our main goal is to make possible a personal relationship with the Lord through a faithful listening of the Word of God and a celebration of the sacraments accompanied by a rich community life.

Our formation period is demanding, but it will turn you into a man, a Christian, an apostle of Christ, serving the Church in the midst of a world in seach of real values.

If you long for holiness, do not hesitate to contact us. You may become one of us.

(Addresses on next page.)

**Canada**
P. François Lapointe, omv
5959, boul. Monk
Montréal (Québec) H4E 3H5
Canada
Tel.: (1) 514-767-7758

**Italy**
P. Andrea Brustolon, omv
Via Malone, 19
10154 Torino
Italia
Tel.: (39) 11-248-2816

**United States**
P. Peter Grover, omv
Our Lady of Grace Seminary
1105 Boylston St.
Boston, MA 02215
U.S.A.
Tel.: (1) 617-266-5999 / 266-5541

**Brasil**
P. Marciu, omv
C.P. 198
13200-970 Jundiai (SP)
Brasil
Tel.: (55) 11-437-0151

**France**
P. Georges Pelletier, omv
7, rue Gentil-Bernard
92260 Fontenay-aux-Roses
France
Tel.: (33) 1-41-13-37-00

**Austria**
P. Tom Kleinschmidt, omv
Burgenland
2443 Loretto
Austria
Tel.: (43) 2255-82-56

**Argentina**
P. Julio Cura, omv
Pedro Goyena 1990
1712 Castelar (B)
Argentina
Tel.: (54) 1-629-0413

❆

## SISTERS OF OUR LADY OF MOUNT CARMEL

### FOUNDED IN FLORENCE, ITALY, ON OCTOBER 15, 1854, BY MOTHER MARIA TERESA SCRILLI

It is a contemplative and active order. Our Mother Foundress' concern for the Moral, Christian and Civil instruction and education for youth from their tenderest years through adolescence gave birth to the teaching apostolate of the order. In later years, the need arose to extend our work to include assistance to the sick in hospitals, to elderly in the nursing homes. We are present in mission countries to bring the good news of Jesus to our brothers and sisters. We also serve in the parishes.

"Young people first of all: seek Jesus! Then, we say to you, Love Jesus! And then ask do I choose carmel to serve Christ in my brothers and sisters."

**Canada**
Sisters of Our Lady of Mount Carmel
2700 Jane Street
North York, Ontario M3L 1S4
Canada
Tel.: (1) 416-749-5545

**United States**
Carmelite Sisters
5 Wheatland Street
Peabody, Mass. 01960
U.S.A.
Tel.: (1) 508-531-4733

Sisters of Our Lady of Mount Carmel
2599 Major Mackenzie Dr.
Maple, Ontario L6A 1C6
Canada
Tel.: (1) 905-303-1000

*Italy*
Istituto Di N.S. Del Carmelo
Via Dei Baglioni, 10
00164 Roma
Italia
Tel.: (29) 6-6615-3752

*Poland*
Wola Gulowska
Gm Adamow - Wol. Siedleckie
21 - 481 Wola Gulowska 50
Poland

Casa di Noviziato - ul.
Poznanska, 33
42-200 Czestochowa
Poland
Tel.: (48) 4-834-629581

Sisters of Our Lady of Mt Carmel
4415 Eighth Street, NE
Washington, D.C. 20017
U.S.A.
Tel.: (1) 202-526-9180

*Brazil*
Irmas Nossa Senhora Do Carmo
Runa Rosarinho, 182
Bairro Sao José
69085 - 070 Mannaus AM
Brazil
Tel.: (55) 92-248-1031

*Czech Republic*
Sestry Karmelita'nky
Lidecko 122
75612 Horni Lidec
Czech Republic
Tel.: (42)-657-98202

*India*
Mother of Carmel Convent
S. Kalamassery - 683104
Kochin, Kerala
S. India
Tel.: (91) 484-54-1004

❊

## LITTLE SISTERS OF THE HOLY FAMILY

### FOUNDED IN MEMRAMCOOK (NEW BRUNSWICK), ON MAY 31, 1880, BY BLESSED MARIE-LÉONIE PARADIS AND TRANSFERRED IN SHERBROOKE (QUÉBEC) IN 1895

United in fraternal communities, in Jesus' name, we give our life joyfully for the spiritual and material support of priests. Inspired by the Holy Family of Nazareth, we unite contemplation to action.

The Church needs you to continue its mission. If you wish to meet this challenge, you can contact us.

*Canada*
General administration
1820, rue Galt Ouest
Sherbrooke (Québec) J1K 1H9
Canada
Tel.: (1) 819-823-0345
Fax: (1) 819-562-2578

*Honduras*
Central house
Prolong. de 12 Calle Norte 3720
Tegucigalpa D.C.
Honduras
Tel. / fax: 504-30-3201

(Continued on next page.)

**United States**
661 North River Road
Manchester N.H. 03104-1955
U.S.A.
Tel.: (1) 603-624-1827

**Guatemala**
Apartado 151
Guatemela Ciudad
Guatemala
Tel.: (502) 2-0476-2419

❊

## SISTERS OF PROVIDENCE

Our charism: to alleviate human misery, whatever shape it may take. Our mission: to be the heart of the Providence in the world, especially to our most underprivileged brothers.

If you want to serve Jesus, to love him in the poor, and to be a witness of the Providence of God, write to us or come see us.

Sisters of Providence
12055, rue Grenet
Montréal (Québec) H4J 2J5
Canada

❊

## THE RECLUSE SISTERS

### CONTEMPLATIVE INSTITUTE

The Recluse Sisters are centered on the mystery of the Eucharist in a life of adoration and intercession.

Their call is embodied in a monastic way of life totally dedicated to seeking God in solitude and silence, in constant prayer and communal sharing, in work and joyful penance.

Their contemplative life remains their fundamental apostolate; it is their specific way of being missionaries at the heart of the Church.

In accordance with monastic tradition, the Recluse Sisters make concrete their service to the Church, particularly in hospitality. They welcome those seeking an oasis of silence and prayer; they share liturgical prayer and silent adoration before the Blessed Sacrament permanently exposed in their monasteries.

Three houses in Canada:

**Canada**
Mother house
12050, boul. Gouin Est
Montréal (Québec) H1C 1B8
Canada
Tel.: (1) 514-648-6801
Fax: (1) 514-643-1836

2351, boul. Labelle
Lafontaine (Québec) J7Z 5T5
Canada
Tel.: (1) 514-438-1852
Fax: (1) 514-565-4593

The Recluse Sisters
Box 51431 S.S. #3
St. Johns (NFLD) A1B 4M2
Canada
Tel. / fax: (1) 709-437-1243

# REDEMPTORISTS

*There is no lack of work !*

Are you wondering about your life direction?
Are you asking how to find a new meaning in your life?

**The Redemptorist community** offers you a life full of challenges
by using your talents in the service of Christ and others. We are ready to take
you on **in a life-style and a work that demand dynamism, audacity and generosity.**

Our life of fellowship, prayer and service proclaims a fundamental belief:
*Jesus Christ is living among us!*

We are more than 6,000 Redemptorists working in about sixty countries..

**Write to us! We will send you more information about us!**

*Yes, in our life-style there is no lack of work!*

*for a*
*living Word!*

**Canada** (French)
Équipe de la pastorale vocationnelle
Résidence Saint-Rédempteur
4957 rue Honoré-Beaugrand
Saint-Augustin (Québec) G3A 1T8
Canada
Tel.: (1) 418-872-3458
Fax: (1) 418-872-6916

**France**
Provincial House
170, boul. du Montparnasse
75014 Paris
France
Tel.: (33) 1-40-64-57-00
Fax: (33) 1-40-47-67-38

**England**
Provincial House
8 Clapham Park Road
Clapham Common
London SW4 7AP
England
Tel.: (44) 171- 622-2793
Fax: (44) 171- 627-3153

**Canada** (English)
Provincial House
426 St. Germain Avenue
Toronto, Ontario M5M 1W7
Canada
Tel.: (1) 416-789-3217
Fax: (1) 416-789-9266

**United States**
Vocation office
St. Alphonsus Residence
22-04 Parsons Blvd.
Whitestone, NY 11357
U.S.A.
Tel.: (1) 718-321-1394
Fax: (1) 718-321-1246

**Italy**
General government
Via Merulana, 31
C.P. 2458
00185 Roma
Italia
Tel.: (39) 6 49 490-1
Fax: (39) 6 446-6012

# Sisters of St. Chrétienne

## Founded in 1807 by Anne-Victoire Tailleur-Méjanès

Sisters of St. Chretienne, we are founded for a mission, namely, like Nina "the Christian", to proclaim Jesus Christ by our whole life, to bring about a world of justice and peace, and to announce the Good News of the Father's love and mercy to all, especially to the lowly and the poor.

If you have a deep desire to follow Christ and to participate in his mission, here or in distant lands... If you wish to live your life fully... If you like to take on challenges... Then come!

### Canada
Provincial House
2375, av. Robert-Giffard # 10
Beauport (Québec) G1E 4H1
Canada
Tel.: (1) 418-663-0532
Fax: (1) 418-663-2783

John D'Or Prairie
Box 608 Alberta T0H 1N0
Canada
Tel.: (1) 403-759-3891
Fax: (1) 403-759-2198

### France
Mother House
60, rue Dupont des Loges
57000 Metz
France
Tel.: (33) 3-87-36-57-03
Fax: (33) 3-87-75-18-81

### Austria
Regional House
Hocstrasse 8
A-1238 Wien-Rodaun
Austria
Tel.: (43) 1-888-41-43-49

### Africa
Rwanda-Zaïre
B.P. 242 Kigali
Rwanda
Tel. / fax: 250-747-59

Djibouti
Foyer social Boulaos
B.P. 2084 Djibouti
Tel.: 253-42-61-76

### United States
Provincial House
297 Arnold Street
Wrentham, MA
U.S.A.
Tel.: (1) 508-384-7841
Fax: (1) 508-384-3170

❄

# Salesians of Don Bosco

### 1947-1997 – 50th Anniversary of presence in Canada

In the Church, we want to be signs and bearers of the love of God for young people, especially those who are poor.

We educate by evangelizing and evangelize by educating.

In the footsteps of Don Bosco, come bring Christ to the young and the young to Christ.

For more information, please contact:

Fr. Richard Authier, s.d.b.
510 Quebec St.
Sherbrooke (Québec) J1H 3L8
Canada
Tel.: (1) 819-562-0053
Fax: (1) 819-565-8872

❈

# Sisters of Saint Jeanne d'Arc

## Founded on December 25th, 1914,
### by F. Marie-Clément Staub, a.a.

Daughters of God through our baptismal consecration and members of his people, we have been chosen by the Spirit and brought to live together in a communal life in order to remind all of our brothers and sisters of the love of Jesus through a life entirely devoted to serving the priests: life of prayer and life given, life of apostleship through collaborative work with the clergy.

The Virgin Mary is the perfect model of our spiritual and apostolic life and we call upon her by the name of Queen of the Clergy.

Saint Jeanne d'Arc is our inspiration, our model of courage, generosity and joy in carrying out our vocation.

God has given you the world, you have been granted a big and generous heart – maybe you will find among us a place to respond to and live your calling!

*Canada*
Mother House
1505, av. de l'Assomption
Sillery (Québec) G1S 4T3
Canada
Tel.: (1) 418-527-2589
Fax: (1) 418-527-7881

*United States*
Notre Dame Rectory
529 Eastern Avenue
Fall River, Ma 02723-2420
U.S.A.
Tel.: (1) 508-675-8582

❈

# Sisters of Saint Francis of Assisi of Lyon

## Founded in Lyon in 1838 by Anne Rollet (S. Agnès-de-la-Conception)

"Love is not loved!" This heartfelt cry by Francis of Assisi resonated in the heart of Anne Rollet, a simple worker from Lyon (France), and its echo is still strongly felt today.

To form a Community of brothers and friends, to live according to the Gospel, to cooperate together more and more in accomplishing God's work, to manifest all around oneself the love and tenderness of the Father, this is the way each of us responds to his personal calling and accomplishes his mission in the world of God today.

Our specific mission engages us in looking after the sick and the old, educating the young, pastoral service and taking care of the underprivileged. We are sensitive to all human suffering, continuing the spiritual gift of our foundress in the inspiration of the Franciscan spirituality characteristic of our order.

If you are in need of giving love and being loved, if you want to share and spread hope and joy around you, we are here to help you. Come and join us!

*Canada*
General administration
2700, rue Lacordaire
Montréal (Québec) H1N 2M6
Canada
Tel.: (1) 514-254-4158
Fax: (1) 514-251-2730

Provincial administration
600, 60ᵉ Rue Est
Charlesbourg (Québec) G1H 3A9
Canada
Tel.: (1) 418-628-2539/418-628-7260
Fax: (1) 418-626-3445

*France*
Mother House
17, rue Rast-Maupas
69001 Lyon
France
Tel.: (33) 4-78-27-13-15
Fax: (33) 4-72-07-97-10

*Haiti*
Provincial administration
Avenue N, n° 33, C.P. 1054
Port-au-Prince
Haiti
Tel.: (509) 45-2344
Fax: (509) 45-3244

❊

# FEDERATION OF SISTERS OF ST. JOSEPH OF CANADA

### "THE LOVE OF CHRIST HAS GATHERED US TOGETHER AS ONE."

Nearly 350 years ago, the first Sisters of St. Joseph began walking through the city of Le Puy, France, educating the poor, caring for the sick, providing shelter for widows and orphans. They went where there were needs, loving the "dear neighbour" and working to make the Good News of Jesus a reality. Today the needs still exist and you will find us with refugees, women in need, disabled children, youth, the elderly, in parishes, schools, retreat and spirituality centres, in offices, hospitals and soup kitchens, serving the People of God in Canada and beyond.

Like our first Sisters, we live together simply, we share prayers and work, laughter and leisure, we pledge our lifelong support to one another for the sake of the reign of God.

In prayer, we seek to listen attentively, to move where the Spirit leads us, and to respond to the movement of grace.

We believe that Jesus continues to walk with us, and we live in hope that our combined efforts will contribute to the transformation of the earth.

We offer our energies and talents for the task of uniting person with person, persons with the earth, and persons with God. We strive to do this in a spirit of gentleness, joy and peace.

We invite you to join us in the journey, to share with us your ideals, visions and dreams, and we will happily share all that we are and all that we are becoming... with you.

For further information please contact:

Sisters of St. Joseph of Toronto
3377 Bayview Avenue
Willowdale, Ontario M2M 3S4
Canada
Tel.: (1) 416-222-1101
Fax: (1) 416-222-9816
E-mail: sisters@idirect.com

Sisters of St. Joseph of London
Box 487
London, Ontario N6A 4X3
Canada
Tel.: (1) 519-432-3781
Fax: (1) 519-432-8557
E-mail: csjlondon@wwdc.com

Sisters of St. Joseph of Pembroke
1127 Pembroke Street West
Pembroke, Ontario K8A 5R3
Canada
Tel.: (1) 613-732-3694
Fax: (1) 613-732-1788
E-mail: stjosfmh@renc.igs.net

Sisters of St. Joseph of Hamilton
Box 155, L.C.D. #1
Hamilton, Ontario L8L 7V7
Canada
Tel.: (1) 905-528-0138
Fax: (1) 905-528-8883
E-mail: akarges@interlynx.net

Sisters of St. Joseph of Peterborough
P.O. Box 566
Peterborough, Ontario K9J 6Z6
Canada
Tel.: (1) 705-745-1307
Fax: (1) 705-745-1377

Sisters of St. Joseph of Sault St. Marie
2025 Main Street West
North Bay, Ontario P1B 2X6
Canada
Tel.: (1) 705-474-3800
Fax: (1) 705-495-3028
E- mail: csjnbay@onlink.net

❋

# SISTERS OF SAINT JOSEPH OF SAINT HYACINTHE

*Our Origins:* Our congregation was founded by the venerable Élisabeth Bergeron, upon the request of the Blessed Louis-Zéphirin Moreau, on the 12th of September 1877, in an abandoned school house in the village of La Providence in the diocese of Saint-Hyacinthe, Quebec.

*The foundation of our spiritual house:* Like Joseph and following the example of Élisabeth Bergeron, the never-ending search of the will of God.

*Our spiritual gift:* We share, along with the majority of communities which were founded in the 19th century, a gift of service and gospel. Our particular way of living it: walking in the footprints of Joseph, the Pilgrim, on a path of incarnation and openness to the world, through the education of youth and families as well as by the evangelization of the poor.

*The spirit which guides us:* That of the Holy Family of Nazareth. That is where we learn the simple virtues that we must make our own: simplicity of a life united by love; joy in communication and brotherly communion; willingness to do God's work in order to better serve his people, and, finally, humility leading us to the weak and poor. Our initials (S.J.S.H.) remind us of: Simplicity, Joy, Service, Humility.

*Our mission:* Our mission takes on all of its significance in these words spoken by Jesus: "In so far as you did this to one of the least of these brothers of mine, you did it to me." (Matt. 25:40). As educators, we teach of a God who is close to all human beings.

*Locations:* Our community includes members from different regions of Canada (Quebec and Manitoba); in Africa (Lesotho, Republic of South Africa; Chad); in Latin America (Brazil and Haiti).

If you wish to receive more information, please communicate with us at one of the following addresses:

## Canada
General administration
805, rue Raymond
Saint-Hyacinthe (Québec) J2S 5T9
Canada
Tel.: (1) 514-773-6067
Fax: (1) 514-773-8044

Regional House
803-15, Arden Ave.
Winnipeg (Manitoba) R2M 2J8
Canada
Tel.: (1) 204-255-4112
Fax: (1) 204-256-1462

## Haiti
Abricots
77 Jubilé Jérémie
Haiti

## Lesotho
Regional House
P.O. Boîte postale 120
Mokhotlong 500
Lesotho
Tel.: 266-92-0290

## Chad
Collège Notre-Dame-du-Tchad
B.P. 61
Moundou
Chad
Tel.: 235-69-12-77

## Brazil
Avenida Joao Pessoa, 387
Filipinho
65 040 001 Sao Luis,
Maranhao, Brazil
Tel.: (55) 98-243-8006
Fax: (55) 98-243-7491

❈

# SISTERS OF ST. JOSEPH OF ST. VALLIER

FOUNDED IN SAINT-VALLIER (FRANCE) IN 1683. WE ARE A BRANCH OF THE GREATER CONGREGATION OF SAINT JOSEPH FOUNDED IN PUY-EN-VELAY (FRANCE), IN 1650, UNDER THE INSPIRATION OF FATHER JEAN-PIERRE MÉDAILLE, JESUIT, AND MGR HENRI DE MAUPAS, BISHOP OF THE PUY

You are creative and daring, you hear the calls, even the silent ones, of people in need, you feel that you are called to build a fairer and more human world: then if you want to discern this calling and be a sign of God's love, you can contact us.

*Canada*
General administration
860, av. Louis-Fréchette
Québec (Québec) G1S 3N3
Canada
Tel.: (1) 418-683-9653
Fax: (1) 418-681-8781

*Haiti*
District House
rue 20-0
C.P. 32
Cap-Haïtien
Haiti
Tel. / fax: (509) 62-09-43

*France*
District House
26240 Saint-Vallier
France
Tel.: (33) 4-75-23-00-20
Fax: (33) 4-75-23-12-23

�֎

## Société de Marie Réparatrice

### Founded in 1857 in Strasbourg, France, by Émilie d'Oultremont, the Baroness of Hooghvorst, a widowed mother of four children (Mother Mary of Jesus)

Dedicated to the restoration through Mary, the Congregation will have the joy of witnessing, on October 12 of this year, Mother Mary of Jesus proclaimed blessed by His Holiness Pope John Paul II.

Following Jesus and just as the Virgin Mary, the Sisters of Marie Réparatrice wish to tell the world of the tenderness of God towards a humanity hurting from sin, evil and suffering. They accomplish this through prayer before the Holy Sacrament and through apostolic activities such as retreats, catechesis, pastoral work, etc.

*Italy*
Mother House
Via Dei Lucchesi 3
00187 Roma
Italia
Tel.: (39) 6-679-2017

*Canada*
Provincial House
1190, rue Guy
Montréal (Québec) H3H 2L4
Canada
Tel.: (1) 514-931-6468

House of Retreat
1025, boul. Mont-Royal Ouest
Outremont (Québec) H2V 2H4
Canada
Tel.: (1) 514-279-5619

✧

# Congregation of the Holy Ghost (the Spiritans)

FOUNDED IN 1703 BY CLAUDE POULLART DES PLACES. IN 1848, IT WAS UNITED WITH THE SOCIETY OF THE HOLY HEART OF MARY, ESTABLISHED BY FRANÇOIS LIBERMANN, A JEW CONVERTED TO CATHOLICISM AND A MYSTIC WHOSE WRITINGS ARE STILL A SOURCE OF INSPIRATION FOR HIS FOLLOWERS.

Spiritans strive to follow in the wake of Christ, seeking the ways of the Holy Spirit within the world and taking Mary as their model. Their motto, "One heart and one soul." Simplicity of life and outlook, openness to others and readiness to serve are genuine elements of the Spiritan character.

Their main aim is to spread the Gospel among the poor. Consequently, they go to meet people and groups of various cultures (they are indeed missionaries), particularly those whose needs are the greatest, as well as the oppressed. Thus, they have been drawn to care for marginalized groups like refugees, to establish schools for young people, centres for orphans, etc. They also accept to take upon themselves various tasks which rather few within the Church are ready to uphold.

They vow to live a life marked by chastity, poverty and obedience as a testimony to the Kingdom of God which is already in our midst while yet still to come. With a view to mutual help, they join in communities where brotherhood and prayer hold a predominant place. Spiritans are present in 54 countries all over the world.

To get in touch with the Spiritans:

*France*
Provincial House
30, rue Lhomond
75005 Paris
France
Tel.: (33) 1-47-07-49-09

*Canada*
Provincial House
9110, av. Papineau
Montréal (Québec) H2M 2C8
Canada
Tel.: (1) 514-384-5238

❇

# Order of the Most Holy Trinity (the Trinitarians)

FOUNDED IN 1198 BY SAINT JOHN OF MATHA AND SAINT FÉLIX OF VALOIS AND REFORMED IN 1599 BY SAINT JOHN BAPTIST OF THE CONCEPTION.

Members of this religious order wear the red and blue cross. They were founded in order to buy back captives imprisoned because of their faith. Today, members of this order work with the underprivileged such as: people living in the streets, alcoholics, drug addicts, and even prisoners. They also contribute to a liberation crusade through work in recovery homes and in parishes, in educative institutions, hospitals, and through missionary work in third-world countries.

We work with the great Trinitarian family: brothers (priests and laymen), nuns, monks and the laity for the glory of the Holy Trinity and the liberation of the poor and imprisoned.

If you would like to verify the Trinity's and the poor's calling, communicate with us:

*Italy*
General administration
Via Massimi, 114-C
00136 Roma
Italia

Provincial House
San Crisogono
Piazza Sonnino, 44
00153 Roma
Italia

Provincial House
Via Fontanelle al
Trivio, 34
80141 Naples
Italia

*Canada*
Provincial House
2700, rue Allard
Montréal (Québec)
H4E 2L8
Canada

*Spain*
Provincial House
Echegaray, 30
28014 Madrid
Spain

Provincial House
Plaza del Cristo
de Gracia, 5
14002 Cordoba
Spain

*India*
Holy Trinity Ashram
Laloor
P.O. Aranattukara
Trichur 680618
Kerala State

*United States*
Provincial House
P.O. Box 5742
Pikesville, Maryland
21208-0742
U.S.A.

*Madagascar*
Provincial House
B.P. 7.133
Saovimbahoaka
101 Antananarivo
Madagascar

*Latin America*
Provincial Vicar
El Tejar Casilla 297
Sucre
Bolivia

Provincial Vicar
P.O. Box 525
Isabela
Puerto Rico 00662

Provincial Delegate
Plaza Sta Cruz
Acatlan, 18
Col. Transito
0620 Mexico, D.F.

Trinitarian Seminary
Los Trinitarios
01 901 Guatemala
Guatemala

*France*
General Delegation
9, Villa Molitor
75016 Paris
France

*Autriche*
Haus der Trinitarier
Mexicoplatz, 12
1020 Vienna
Austria

*Trinitarian Sisters*
Granados, 1
23740 Andujar
(Jaen)
Spain

of Valence
17, Chazière
69004 Lyon
France

del Riposo
via Madonna del
Riposo, 71
00165 Roma
Italia

Valencia
Orihuela, 45
46009 Valencia
Spain

Urquijo, 18
Marquès de Urquijo, 18
28008 Madrid
Spain

Majorque
Ausias Marc, 39-1e
08010 Barcelona
Spain

❊

## Ursulines of the Canadian Union

We have chosen to live the Covenant with Christ as his spouses. The Lord nourishes our contemplation, strengthens the communion between us and urges us in our mission of education in the Church.

If you want to experience the joy of giving your life to Christ so that others may receive life, write to us or come see us.

Ursulines of the Canadian Union
1358, rue de Montmorency
Québec (Québec) G1S 2G8
Canada
Tel.: (1) 418-683-0671
Fax: (1) 418-681-4740

❊

## Sisters of Charity of Quebec

Assembled in an apostolic Congregation, we live up to our consecration to God, striving, first of all, to glorify Christ by assisting his suffering members.

Following the teaching of our foundress, Mother Marcelle Mallet, unanimously called by her contemporaries "Good Mother Mallet", we place ourselves under the guidance of the Sacred Heart of Jesus so that our lives be filled by compassion, and thus our service to others be a reflection of his merciful Love.

Be it in Quebec, in the United States, in Japan, in South America, we wish to bring everywhere the Good News that God loves us in Jesus Christ.

*Canada*
General Administration
2655, rue Le Pelletier
Beauport (Québec) G1C 3X7
Canada
Tel.: (1) 418-628-8860

*United States*
Sisters of Charity of Quebec
333 Pawtucket Street
Lowell, MA 01854
U.S.A.
Tel.: (1) 508-441-1696
Fax: (1) 508-453-9585

*Japan*
Quebec Caritas Shudojo Kai
Honbu Shudoin
16-15, Azamino 1 Chome
Aoba-Ku, Yokohama
Japan 225
Tel.: (81) 45-901-8341
Fax: (81) 45-902-1252

*Paraguay*
Hermanas de la Caridad
San Cristobal CC. 1150
Asuncion
Paraguay
Tel.: (595) 21-604-294
Fax: (595) 21-607-907

❊

## Missionary Carmelites

The Missionary Carmelites, one branch of the large Carmelite tree, are the spiritual daughters of the Blessed Francis Palau, a Carmelite priest; Gift of the Holy Spirit! The community is like the offspring from the contemplative and missionary charism which invites us to walk through life with open hands in order to answer preoccupations and to cultivate hope.

Here are the objectives of our spiritual path:

– To live in communion with the Church;
– To be authentic and significant witnesses of the presence of Christ, especially among the most underpriviledged in our mission countries.

The ecclesial charism is the meaning of our mission. It includes: detecting the needs of our brothers and sisters, figuring out what their urgencies are, and finding the creative answers which may bring about their growth and liberation.

Does our choice of life interest you? The Lord awaits you!

The Missionary Carmelites are present in 36 countries.

*Canada*
2797, av. Willowdale
Montréal (Québec) H3T 1H4
Canada
Tel.: (1) 514-737-3224
Fax: (1) 514-286-1732

※

## SAINT PAUL SOCIETY

### FOUNDED IN ITALY PAR FATHER ALBERIONE

We have a mission of evangelizing by the printed word and by the media. We work in many countries and we will be glad to have you with us if you desire to give your life to God and to your brothers.

Write to us to find out our addresses in other countries.

*Canada*
Pierre Catalano
3965, boul. Henri-Bourassa Est
Montréal (Québec) H1H 1L1
Canada
Tel.: (1) 514-322-7344

You, our youth, are the present and the future of the Church. All of you are called upon by the Lord to live in the ways of Jesus.

In marriage, in consecrated life, in priesthood, be a shining light for others to follow!

† *Jacques Berthelet, c.s.v.*
*Bishop of Saint-Jean-Longueuil*

## Other contributors to this project...

Mgr Maurice Couture, archevêque de Québec
Mgr Pierre Morissette, évêché de Baie-Comeau
Père François Breton, Fraternité sacerdotale, Montréal
Abbaye cistercienne d'Oka
Mme Thérèse Sauvageau, Grondines
M. Eugène Talbot, Québec
Dom Vidal, Saint-Benoît-du-Lac
Mgr André Gaumont, archidiocèse de Sherbrooke
Abbé Denis Duval
Abbé André Lessard
Mgr Eugène P. LaRocque, Cornwall (Ont.)
Mgr Adam Exner, archidiocèse de Vancouver
M. Marc Delisle
M. Rémi Marcoux
Moniales bénédictines, Mont-Laurier
Abbaye cistercienne de Saint-Romuald
Religieuses de Notre-Dame-du-Sacré-Cœur, Dieppe (N.-B.)
Filles de Jésus, Rimouski
Mme Madeleine Galibois
Sœurs de l'Institut Jeanne d'Arc, Ottawa (Ont.)
Trappe Notre-Dame, Mistassini
Mgr Jean Gratton, évêché de Mont-Laurier
Séminaire de Québec
Mgr Joseph Baril, Roman Catholic Episcopal Corporation of Labrador
Sisters of Charity, Halifax (N.-É.)
Mgr François Thibodeau, évêché d'Edmunston
Filles de la Providence, Prince Albert (Sask.)
Abbé Roger Chabot
Mgr Ernest Léger, archevêché de Moncton (N.-B.)
Filles de la Sagesse, Edmonton (Alberta)
Missionnaires Oblates de Saint-Boniface, Québec
Mgr Raymond Dumais, évêché de Gaspé
Cardinal Louis-Albert Vachon, Québec
Filles de la Sagesse, Montréal
Mgr Gérard Drainville, évêché d'Amos
Mgr Clément Fecteau, évêché de Sainte-Anne-de-la-Pocatière
Mgr Bertrand Blanchet, évêché de Rimouski
M. Pierre Péladeau
M. Louis Garneau
Sœurs de la Sainte-Famille de Bordeaux
**Conférence des évêques catholiques du Canada**